FROM SUNDAY SCHOOL TO CHURCH SCHOOL

Continuities in Protestant
Church Education in the
United States, 1860-1929

Jack L. Seymour

UNIVERSITY
PRESS OF
AMERICA

ACKNOWLEDGMENTS

The support and encouragement of several people
needs to be gratefully acknowledged: Charles Foster,
Frank Gulley, Stephen Schmidt, Robert Thomson, and
Jack Willers have all read sections of the manuscript
and discussed my conclusions; Dorothy Parks and Albert
Hurd assisted me in uncovering resources long buried in
archives; and Sharon Cates, Sue Detterman, Linda
Prather, and Loretta Roland have helped with typing and
proofreading. I also need to thank my family who supported me through four years of research and writing.

TABLE OF CONTENTS

v

INTRODUCTION

Christian religious education as a field of study seems to be emerging from an eclipse. A new sense of hopefulness is seen in the contemporary attention to the future of Christian education. A crisis of identity has been recognized and has resulted in an exciting search for new directions.

At present, significant reflection on alternative approaches to Christian education is taking place. One task force of professors is seeking to clarify how Christian education is an academic discipline. The relationships of Christian education to public education, Christian theology, and the church are thus being examined.[1] Others are seeking to organize the various theories of Christian education and to clarify their differences.[2] For example, the differences among approaches that emphasize education as instruction, socialization, or empowerment are being considered.

These developments reflect a mood in contrast to that of the late 1960s and early 1970s when church educators suggested that their profession was in a serious crisis. At that time, both Protestant and Catholic educators sought a new identity for the field of Christian education.[3] Robert Lynn, a historian of the American Sunday School movement, argued that the identity which had informed the field had waned. Correspondingly, Berard Marthaler, the commentator on the Catholic General Cathechetical Directory, called for a "re-visionist catechetics" which transcended past formulations of Christian education theory.

Today that search for identity has inspired scholarship, yet anxiety still exists about whether the new research will have a substantial effect on the church. Much of the research seems inconsistent. Some persons, for example, emphasize that the church has depended too heavily on the study of education for its theory and methods, while others state that the church has not adequately embodied that which it has appropriated from public education.[4] There is also conflict about the role theology is to play in Christian education.

Clearly research is needed to clarify some of the potential directions for Christian education. Not only is it necessary to examine empirically the adequacy of the new approaches suggested for Christian education, but also historical research is necessary on how the present situation was shaped and on what approaches have been suggested in the past. Many convictions about education in the church as well as issues and answers which confront Christian educators can be traced to past decisions about the purpose, form, and scope of the church's educational ministry.

This study is to be a step toward uncovering the convictions and assumptions at the core of Christian religious education. The thesis is that policy decisions which were made at a critical time in the life of the Sunday school (1830-1900), when the focus of the Sunday school was shifted from an institution concerned with the education and evangelization of poor and frontier children to one concerned with the training of the children of the faithful in the religion of the church, have become enduring assumptions which form and judge the practice of Christian education today.[5]

The thesis of this study challenges the prevailing understanding of the history of the American Sunday school movement in which a sharp contrast is drawn between the nineteenth century Sunday school and the twentieth century church school. The common interpretation of the church's educational ministry holds that the major transition took place at the turn of the century when church education became a profession and drew heavily on the discipline of education for its theory and method. Agreements made and styles developed during the progressive era are thought to set the context for present decisions about Christian religious education.

The prevailing interpretation divides Sunday school history into six periods with three before 1900 and three after.[6] The first is dated from approximately 1780 to 1830 and is called the Sunday school as missionary and philanthropic agency. Here the Sunday school is understood as an educational agency, only sometimes connected to the church, concerned with the religious, moral, and "public" education of the young.

Between 1830 and 1860 the Sunday school was in transition moving from an extra-church agency to a church institution concerned with the evangelization and nurture of the young. During that period, the

viii

purpose of the Sunday school was questioned. Its task
of providing basic education was being taken over by
common schools and significant questions were raised
about the role of religion in education. From the
churches which had successfully begun to use the Sunday
school as a means of "denominational religious indoctrination" for the children of the church, a new
rationale was found for the Sunday school. It was re-
defined as the "nursery of the church."[7]

The third period, the evangelical Sunday school,
is dated from approximately 1860 to 1900. It is a time
when the nursery of the church was solidified. Robert
Lynn calls this period the "old-time" school. It is
one in which a pan-denominational group committed to
evangelical faith sought to extend the Sunday school as
the major religious unifying and reforming factor in
American life.[8] It was a period of great expansion and
enthusiasm where the evangelical spirit of the revival
became rooted in the Sunday school as the primary agent
of church growth. The basic theological tenets of this
period were those Martin Marty of the University of
Chicago Divinity School has termed "the righteous
empire"--consisting of convictions that the Protestant
evangelical faith would be able to ". . . attract the
allegiance of all the people, to develop a spiritual
kingdom, and to shape the nation's ethos, mores,
manners, and often its law."[9] The Sunday school was a
primary institution in this "empire."

In 1903 the fourth period, that of progressive
religious education, is thought to have been born with
the creation of the Religious Education Association.
As a prevailing force, this period extended until 1929
with the depression, but it continued to have some
influence into the 1940s and 1950s. This period, called
by Lynn the "new-time" school, is characterized by its
allegiance, on the one hand, to liberal Protestant
thought with its commitment to the principles of divine
immanence, growth, the goodness of persons, and the
historical Jesus; and, on the other hand, to progressive education theory represented most clearly in the
experimental and democratic philosophy of John Dewey.[10]
This is the period that is commonly thought to be the
one of significant change when the Sunday school in
becoming the church school set the context for modern
Christian religious education; for during its years,
the discipline of religious education was founded and
was linked to research in psychology and education.

Dated with the depression, a period of theological reconstruction is thought to have emerged. Based on neo-orthodox theology and critical of the liberalism of progressive religious education, the educators emphasized the Christian content and character of their work, and focused more heavily on the church as the agent of Christian education.11 For them, the school was valid only as the school of the church. A later commentator on this shift in Christian education, Randolph Crump Miller, now Professor Emeritus of Christian Education at Yale University Divinity School, characterized this era as one of theological reconstruction.

> It took a theological analysis to put Christian education back on the right track. This was resented among some educators who had not kept abreast of theological developments or who were not theologians in any real sense. . . . A sociology of education is not sufficient to provide a social theology of Christian education.12

The neo-orthodox educators characterized the progressive period as non-theological.

Finally, the contemporary period begins in the mid-1960s with a decline in church school enrollments and the search for new methods, procedures, and theologies to undergird and focus the church's work of education. This period can be characterized as a search for a new identity. A variety of educational and theological styles are present.

While accepting much of the above periodization, in contrast to the prevailing belief, this study reflects the conviction that the context for present-day Christian education was set in the period of redefinition and embodied in the period of the evangelical Sunday school in mainline Protestantism. The key issues--its purpose, its relationship to education, and the scope of its activities--were formulated in the middle of the nineteenth century, and influenced not only the progressive period, but present Christian education.

Throughout the history of the interpretation of Protestant church education, there have been hints at this thesis. For example, Hugh Hartshorne, the director of the Institute of Social and Religious Research of Yale University in the 1930s, suggested a complementary assessment in his empirical analysis of ten outstanding church educational programs. Hartshorne found basic contradictions in the churches between an expressed progressive theory of Christian education and an antiquated practice. Even the best church schools, he concluded, were still controlled by traditional assumptions.

> The process of accretion whereby the traditional school has been broadened and enlarged its work seems to have effected little change in the underlying historic assumptions; in fact, the acceptance of innovation has depended largely upon their probable worth as agencies for strengthening and perpetuating the accepted stereotypes.[13]

The search for these traditional assumptions which have controlled the development of Protestant Christian education is significant to the present search for a new identity for the discipline.

As a revisionist interpretation of the Sunday school, this study argues that understanding the continuities between the Sunday school of the nineteenth century and the church school of the twentieth is essential to understanding the framework within which contemporary Protestant church education functions.

To examine the presence of continuity in the development of the church's school, an assessment must be made of the self-understandings reflected by key Christian education theorists in the two important periods of the evangelical Sunday school, 1860-1900, when the basic self-understanding was solidified, and the progressive period of religious education, 1903-1929, when most interpreters have thought the structure of the church's education was significantly altered. The selection of these periods allows for an identification of the structure of the church's education and its development.

For the period from 1860-1900, the works of John Vincent, a Methodist pastor and Sunday school leader, and of Edward Eggleston, an editor of interdenominational curriculum, are examined. Both were Sunday school reformers who differed on the directions for

Christian education. Vincent agreed with the new direction emerging for the church's education while Eggleston argued that the redefinition had forgotten the mission agenda of the Sunday school, that it enforced uniformity, and that it substituted an educational base for a religious one.

For the progressive period the work of Henry Cope, the general secretary of the new Religious Education Association from 1907-1922, and that of George Albert Coe, the predominant theorist of progressive religious education will be used as illustrations. While Cope and Coe were in substantial theoretical agreement, Coe moved beyond the church focus of many other progressive religious educators and advocated a more public, community context for religious education.

From a comparison of the answers of these key leaders and critics to the basic question of the Sunday school as to its purpose and method, the "reality-base" of church school education can then be uncovered, the enduring issues isolated, and the major challenges which were ignored highlighted. Through the analysis, issues for the future of Christian religious education will be suggested.

Notes

[1] Allen J. Moore, ed., Report of the Task Force on Defining the Academic Discipline of Religious Education, 2 vols. (Nashville: The Board of Discipleship of The United Methodist Church, 1980).

[2] Jack L. Seymour and Donald E. Miller, eds., Contemporary Approaches to Christian Education (Nashville: Abingdon, 1982).

[3] Robert Lynn, "A Little More 'Know-Why," Please," in A Colloquy on Christian Education, ed. John H. Westerhoff III (Philadelphia: Pilgrim Press, 1972), pp. 180-187; and Berard Marthaler, "Towards a Revisionist Model in Catechetics (Reflections on David Tracy's Blessed Rage for Order)," Living Light 13 (Fall 1976):458, 468-469.

[4]John Westerhoff III, Will Our Children Have Faith? (New York: Seabury Press, 1976), pp. 38-42, 49-50; and James Michael Lee, "Toward a New Era: A Blueprint for Positive Action," in The Religious Education We Need, ed. James Michael Lee (Misawaka, IN: Religious Education Press, 1977), pp. 112-122.

[5]This study focuses on mainline Protestantism, those denominations which used the Sunday school primarily, the Congregational church, the Methodist churches, the Baptist churches, and the Presbyterian churches. Some other Protestant bodies like the Lutherans opted for a parochial school system rather than the Sunday school.

[6]For an understanding of this periodization see Robert W. Lynn and Elliott Wright, The Big Little School: The Sunday Child of American Protestantism (New York: Harper & Row, 1971); Boardman Kathan, ed. "Pioneers of Religious Education in the 20th Century: A Festschrift for Herman E. Wornom," Religious Education 73 (Special Edition, September-October 1978); and John Westerhoff III, Who Are We? The Quest for a Religious Education (Birmingham, AL: Religious Education Press, 1978).

[7]Anne M. Boylan, "'The Nursery of the Church:' Evangelical Protestant Sunday Schools, 1820-1880" (Ph.D. dissertation, University of Wisconsin, 1973), p. 2.

[8]Lynn and Wright, Big Little School, pp. 56-79.

[9]Martin E. Marty, Righteous Empire: The Protestant Experience in America (New York: Dial Press, 1970), foreward.

[10]Lynn and Wright, Big Little School, pp. 77-94. For a theological criticism of this period see H. Shelton Smith, Faith and Nurture (New York: Charles Scribner's Sons, 1941), pp. 4-32.

[11]These themes are developed in many places. A primary example is Smith, Faith and Nurture.

[12]Randolph Crump Miller, "Christian Education as a Theological Discipline and Method," Religious Education 48 (November-December 1953):409.

[13]Hugh Hartshorne and Earle V. Ehrhardt, Church Schools of Today (New Haven: Yale University Press, 1933), p. 218.

CHAPTER I

INTERPRETATIONS OF THE DEVELOPMENT
OF CHURCH EDUCATION

The story of the development of the Sunday school and of church education is still largely untold. There has been a lack of historical research on church education. Because of this fact, it is not surprising that there is such a crisis of identity in Christian religious education. Historical research is a primary way of understanding the identity of a people or institution.

Recently, some public school and church historians have advocated such historical work. Lawrence Cremin, the President of Teacher's College in New York City, has argued that the Sunday school has been a profound part of America's public education and has not been fully understood because of the lack of research.[1] Robert Lynn has also received support from church historians when he suggested that ". . . the Sunday school still offers contemporary Protestants a way to understand both their own religious heritage and the history of social movements in this country. . . . This 'purloined letter' is ripe and ready for discovery and critical examination."[2] The church's educational program has been a significant part of the American educational system and a major social institution whose story must be explored, not only to assist the church in clarifying its educational mission, but also to assist the culture in understanding its educational system.

In the last fifteen years, some new understandings of the history of the church's educational program have begun to emerge which offer insights into the story of Protestant education.[3] As a result some of the transitions in the history of church education as well as optional directions which the church's educational program could have taken may be clearer.

Most of these interpretations support the prevailing thesis that the progressive period was <u>the</u> period of significant change in the life of the Sunday school and is the backdrop for present activity in Christian education. It is thought that the Sunday school became a real school during this period. However, more recently a few studies have begun to challenge the prevailing thesis, examining continuities in Protestant church education which can be dated much earlier into the middle of the nineteenth century.

Before examining these contemporary interpretations, it is important to review the history of interpretations of Protestant church education in America. These alternatives express the self-understandings and definitions of Christian education during the times in which they were written. They also parallel convictions expressed in the history of public education.

Henry Clay Trumbull: The First Interpretive History

The first comprehensive, interpretive history of the Sunday school was published in 1888 by Henry Clay Trumbull. Consisting of his Yale lectures on the Sunday school, The Sunday School: Its Origin, Mission, Methods, and Auxiliaries dealt with far more than history.[4] Trumbull was one of the preeminent leaders and reformers of the Sunday school from the time of the Civil War. A minister, army chaplain, and Sunday school teacher, Trumbull dedicated his life to the development of the Sunday school serving on the highest committees of the American Sunday School Association and its successor, the International Sunday School Association. It was Trumbull's conviction that ". . . the Sunday school is an agency approved of God for the evangelizing and the religious training of the race; and that it is peculiarly and preeminently adapted to the needs of our American communities."[5]

Needless to say, Trumbull was proud of the advance he had seen in the Sunday school. He described the difficulties which the Sunday school faced in being accepted as the church's primary agency for education. To him, while the origin of the Sunday school could be traced to the first Christian century, it was only on the American continent that it found a firm soil.

The Sunday school, in his mind, was exclusively responsible for a religious advance in the nineteenth century, and the renewal of religious (he meant Protestant) faith and of morality.[6] He proudly quoted a study on the instruction of children in America conducted by the French government for the 1876 Centennial Exposition which concluded,

2

The Sunday school is not an accessory agency in
the normal economy of American education; it does
not add a superfluity; it is an absolute necessity
for the complete instruction of .the child. Its
aim is to fill by itself the complex mission which
elsewhere is in large measure assigned to the
family, the school, and the church. . . . All
things . . . unite to assign to this institution
a grand part in the American life. Most diverse
circumstances· cooperate to give it an amplitude,
a solidity, and a popularity which is quite
unique.7

Unlike his successors, Trumbull did not look exclusively to the public school as a model for the
church's educational work. In fact, he clearly suggested that the Sunday school was an impetus to the
development of public school instruction.8 Trumbull
saw the Sunday school as a special agency of the church
which had overcome many obstacles and had become "God's
chosen agency . . . for the evangelizing and for the
instruction of those whom his Church is to reach
and to rear."9 To ignore this purpose or to fulfill it
inadequately was to be unfaithful. His story of the
Sunday school was one of success and triumph in church
education for the benefit of the American public. His
story was retold by many others throughout the twentieth century.

The Sunday School Triumphant Interpretation

The first significant attention given to the history of the church's educational program can be traced
to the early twentieth century. Amidst the progressive
spirit of the time, several books were published to
celebrate and solidify the new enthusiasm directed toward the church's educational ministry. The emergence
of the profession of religious educator, the founding
of new religious education organizations like the
Religious Education Association (REA), and the one-
hundredth anniversary of the American Sunday-School
Union all motivated reflection on the past.

The story told by the progressives is much like
that of Trumbull, but it is clearer in attributing the
real change in church education to progressive innovations. Their story tells of ". . . the evolution of
Sunday school method from the early crudities to the
standardized church school of modern days."10

3

The key works advancing this position were Arlo
Ayres Brown, A History of Religious Education in Recent
Times, published in 1923; Marianna C. Brown, Sunday-
School Movements in America, 1901; Henry Frederick Cope,
The Evolution of the Sunday School, 1911; E. Morris
Fergusson, Historic Chapters in Christian Education in
America: A Brief History of the American Sunday School
Movement, and the Rise of the Modern Church School,
1935; and Edwin Wilbur Rice, The Sunday-School Movement
1780-1917 and the American Sunday-School Union 1817-
1917, 1917.11 While each had different emphases and
represents developing thoughts in the first four decades of the twentieth century, there were common
themes.

Briefly, they argued that significant progress had
occurred throughout the history of Protestant church
education, yet significant development was still needed
if the church was to fulfill its responsibility in the
greater American educational system. The task of
church education was to provide the moral and spiritual
core for the development of the American character.
To do this task required continuing improvement in the
church's educational program, particularly more attention to methods of instruction. It was their conviction that essential and rapid progress was needed.
Anything which interrupted the speed of change was seen
as recalcitrance. They argued that progressive tendencies needed to be enhanced.

Their position paralleled that of the first real
histories of education which were being written at
approximately the same time. Volumes written by Henry
Barnard, Amory Dwight Mayo, Herbert Baxter Adams, Paul
Monroe, and Ellwood Patterson Cubberley told the story
of the common school triumphant which characterized
American educational understandings for the first half
of the twentieth century.12 The story was one of the
triumph of the public school which not only molded the
various immigrant groups of the melting pot into one
people, but also educated persons for and extended
American democracy. The school was seen as the primary
institution for the building of the American character.
School work was seen as the most important contributor
to freedom, rational decision making, democracy and
American culture. It was also their assumption that
American culture was implicitly Christian.

4

The effect of this history of education was to
center attention on the institution of the public school
as the primary American vehicle for education and to
give support to the emerging teaching profession. This
story must, however, be seen as one segment in a larger
matrix of professionalization of American society which
took place during the progressive period.[13] The progressives believed that the complexity of the emerging
industrial order demanded high job expertise and therefore specialization. This professionalization could be
seen in the fields of law, medicine, education, and
even in the ministry. The crucial functions of society,
it was thought, had to be fulfilled in the best possible manner by the most capable persons. The schools,
particularly secondary and higher education, were given
the task of preparing persons to improve the quality of
life, and train them to protect freedom and democracy.

It is therefore not surprising that this cultural
context encouraged those who were interested in the
church's educational task to specialize and professionalize. But even here some basic convictions had to be
honored. The speciality of church educators was of
course in directing the institution of the Sunday
school, and this in turn was intended to contribute to
the wider task of American education. The Sunday
school was thought to be one arm in the grand system of
American education. Where the public school provided
secular training, the Sunday school provided the essential moral and religious training. The Sunday school
was the soul of public education and church educators
experts in spiritual things.

Edwin Rice well represented the Sunday school triumphant position when he introduced his historical
study with statements of the "phenomenal extension" of
the church's educational program: its enlistment of an
army of lay teachers, its production of a vast mass of
religious literature, and its remarkable evangelism
which spread Christianity. Yet, his agenda in writing
a history was to stimulate continuing progress.

But the Sunday school has not yet enlisted the
world in Bible study or Bible reading. Serious
problems and immense tasks still confront the
fulfillment of its high ideals. Though the
institution has passed the experimental stage,
it is yet comparatively in its youthful period.
Its origin and achievements to the present may

5

be chronicled; its history cannot be written while
its great work remains undone. . . . [T]he institution is still making history.[14]

Great progress had occurred, even greater progress was to come, if only educators in the church
would adequately respond: here was the theme of these
historians. Their mood was one of exhilaration and
pride over the history of the Sunday school, of excitement about rapidly emerging new ideas and, yet, of
fear that the exhilaration and enthusiasm would not be
enough to meet a modern age. These historians vacil-
lated between feelings of pride and of crisis.

Significant cultural changes related to war, progress and depression frightened them. They believed
that education in the church had the only chance of
averting a total crisis in civilization. Church education had to empower daily living with a soul. Its
methods of enhancing spiritual growth and building
character had to be strengthened. These .historians
looked to education to find the appropriate methods.[15]

Such an understanding motivated how they viewed
the past. They particularly applauded the past Sunday
school leaders who had had the foresight to insist on
educational improvements. Cope, for example, praised
the "elasticity of response" of the Sunday school which
had ". . . adopted the principle of graded lessons,
recognized the validity of educational principles in
Sunday school work, and prompted the technical training
of ministers for their work in the school."[16]

While praising trends which encouraged progress,
they highlighted the differences between the old-
fashioned Sunday school and the progressive church
school. Theodore Soares, writing in 1928 on the
twenty-fifth anniversary of the founding of REA,
sharply drew the contrast. He claimed that the "devotion, zeal, religious faith," which characterized the
mood of the Sunday school prior to the turn of the century was merely an expression of popular religious
enthusiasm that lacked depth.

Thoughtful leaders felt that the whole movement
was wanting in depth. It lacked body, content,
meaning. It was depending upon excitement rather
than upon understanding and purpose. . . . The
International Sunday School Convention was largely

6

in the hands of promoters and oratorical evangelists, who met all suggestions of educational
procedure with the objection that Christianity
was not an educational but an evangelistic process.[17]

For Soares, the progressive REA provided the alternative with depth.

Soares' conviction was repeated by most of the
historians. Fergusson, for example, called those who
had resisted moves to a graded curriculum the victims
of a "militant Orthodoxy." Marianna Brown concluded
that the Sunday School was not yet a true success,
neither by the standards of education nor the Church.
Cope argued that much of the Sunday school development
had been accidental or incidental.[18]

While telling a story of the success of the
church's educational program and advocating for increased attention to the theory and practice of church
education, the Sunday school triumphant historians
exaggerated the difference between the Sunday school
movement and its stepchild, the church school. The
relationship between the reason for church education,
that is spiritual growth, and the particular form which
it took was overlooked. In most instances, the story
emphasized how the Sunday school inspired public education, how it listened to educational development, and
how much more it needed to be shaped by education, but
it was not totally devoid of the more foundational
question of the purpose of church education. These
historians told their generation to take pride in the
past successes and the present attention on the church's
school, but they also told them of the important work
still to be done. For much of the twentieth century,
this was the message of the historians to Christian
educators.

The Neo-Orthodox Theological Interpretation

The shift of emphasis, thought to have occurred in
the progressive era, was highlighted further by neo-
orthodox Christian educators in the 1930s and 1940s.
However, rather than seeing hope and potential in the
changes suggested by progressive educators, the neo-
orthodox critics thought that the church's educational
ministry had been led in a wrong direction. They

7

thought that the optimism and cultural dependence of the liberals had undercut the centrality of the Christian message and a realistic assessment of human salvation and potential.[19] Neo-orthodox educators highlighted the tradition and its emphasis on doctrines of human sin, the reality of evil and the sovereignty of God.

Clearly distinguishing themselves from the previous educational epoch, these educators emphasized a return to orthodox Christian content. Theologically, their question was how the church's education was faithfully Christian.

Reinhold Niebuhr, the foremost American neo-orthodox theologian, was to argue that liberal education misunderstood the capacity of the human person, whom he saw as both a problem-creator as well as a problem-solver, and the complexity of moral decision making and moral action. Niebuhr thought that the lack of a clear transcendent reference in liberal education made education an instrument of the dominant class and avoided dealing seriously with issues of social change and social justice.[20] He called, as did other neo-orthodox leaders, for a return to the transcendent biblical faith as content and focus of education.

The problem for liberal religious education was further compounded by its apparent lack of effectiveness. Many of the progressive reforms were unrealized. While in its early years, it had resulted in a new graded curriculum, new church school architecture, and the new profession of director of religious education, changes did not seem to continue or to culminate. Two studies conducted by Hugh Hartshorne in the 1920s suggested liberal religious education had neither significantly changed church school practice nor made church persons more moral.[21] In addition, the agenda of liberal religious education to reform curriculum was never completed. The Sub-Committee on International Council of Religious Education proposed in 1928 a new theory for curriculum and defined the research necessary to develop the curriculum; yet even into the 1940s the task had not been completed.[22] The exciting notions of developing curriculum consonant with the actual experience of the pupil, and "as inclusive as life itself" remained unrealized.

Neo-orthodox educators dated liberal religious education from the beginning of the twentieth century. They argued that at that time a significant shift took place in the church's educational ministry with liberal theology and progressive education becoming its two primary sources. H. Shelton Smith, the neo-orthodox critic of liberal religious education, argued that liberal education had sent Christian education on a wrong direction and supported it with an inadequate foundation. He wrote, ". . . contemporary Liberalism as a creed is basically outmoded, and must therefore be critically reconsidered and revised. This means, to be sure, that the theological roots of Liberal Protestant nurture must also be reexamined and reconstructed."[23]

Furthermore, neo-orthodox educators emphasized that the church as the community of faith was the only proper locus for Christian education and therefore a primary role of the minister was that of teacher. They charged that progressive education had resulted in an emphasis on school over church and educator over minister. In addition, they rejected the theory of the progressives which they saw as emphasizing general education theory over theology and the needs of the child over the content of the Christian faith.[24] In retrospect, some of these charges are seen to be unfair; many of the liberals, such as Coe, initiated conversation about the community of faith as the context for religious education which continued in progressives in the International Council of Religious Education.[25] Nevertheless, these charges highlighted the mood of separation which characterized Christian education theory during those decades.

One of the best examples of the contrast drawn by neo-orthodox educators is represented in the Faith and Life Curriculum of the Presbyterian Church, U.S.A. In 1941, the Presbyterian Church withdrew from the graded lesson outline committee of The International Council of Religious Education to embark on the production of a Presbyterian graded curriculum.[26] This action signaled a radical revision in the understanding of curriculum.

The new Presbyterian curriculum departed from many of the ingredients in liberal religious education, particularly the exclusive concern with the needs of the child. Content principles were defined which highlighted the essential elements in the neo-orthodox interpretation of Christian (they would say biblical) faith: that is, the church as a teacher of a revealed faith, the sinfulness and failure of human agency, the sovereignty of God, the person and work of Jesus Christ, the Bible as the document of faith, and the responsibility of Christian Discipleship.[27] To edit their material the Presbyterians selected a neo-orthodox Biblical scholar, James Smart, who emphasized the new directions which this curriculum claimed. He argued, "In many of our churches our education of the younger generation in the Christian faith is so grossly inadequate and ineffective that to continue on the present level is to invite disaster. . . . The Church must, in the fullest sense of the word, become a teaching church.[28] Even more than the liberal historians themselves, the neo-orthodox educators set the liberal progressive period in religious education apart from that which preceded and followed it. It was characterized as inadequate.

The Contemporary Ecological Interpretation

The prevailing contemporary interpretation continues the sharp contrast between the church school of the liberal period and the Sunday school that preceded it. These scholars see present Christian education as set in the progressive era. The church school projected a professional, educational identity while the Sunday school's identity was lay and evangelical. While emphases of contemporary representatives differ, they are in common agreement that the changes brought about in the early twentieth century were not beneficial for the theory and practice of the church's educational work; for the changes professionalized a lay movement, locked religious education into an exclusive relationship with education theory, and ignored the previous ecology of institutions in which the Sunday school had successfully functioned.

This interpretation of church education history has been directly affected by revisions in public school history, particularly by the two books which revolutionized the thinking about American education: Bernard Bailyn, Education in the Forming of American Society, published in 1960 and Lawrence Cremin. The Wonderful World of Ellwood Patterson Cubberly: An Essay on the Historiography of American Education, published in 1965.[29] While Bailyn, an American

10

colonial historian, was the first to challenge the prevailing public school triumphant position, it was Cremin who brought the new position to the forefront.

The predominant convictions of the revisionist public school histories differ sharply from the older public school triumphant position which had provided educators in the first six decades of the twentieth century with an understanding of their task. Cremin and Bailyn attacked its three basic tenets: (a) that American education is defined by the institution of the public school, (b) that the school has moved from the periphery of culture to its center, and (c) that the school and teachers are predominantly responsible for the expansion and protection of American democracy. They claimed that this interpretation of history was guilty of

> . . . the sin of anachronism, by looking for the seeds of the public school in the colonial period; the sin of parochialism, by confusing education with schooling, hence writing a history of the institutional evolution of schools; and the sin of evangelism, by seeking to inspire teachers with professional zeal rather than attempting to understand what really happened.[30]

In contrast, they argued that a proper history of education would seek to understand the various factors which contributed to the education of the American public. For such an understanding, they were convinced that one must look beyond the public schools of the progressive era to the other agencies which also educated the public, that is families, churches, the media, museums, libraries, benevolent societies, industrial training, etc.[31]

Bailyn provided a totally new definition for education beyond that of education-equals-schooling when he suggested that education is ". . . the entire process by which culture transmits itself across the generations."[32] While Bailyn's definition was criticized as too broad--in fact, coequaling enculturation-- it did provide a new way of conceiving of how the American character had been formed. Cremin was to narrow Bailyn's definition and to make it accessible to the discipline of education. Cremin's definition is today generally accepted: education is ". . . the deliberate, systematic, and sustained effort to

11

transmit, evoke, or acquire knowledge, attitudes, values, skills, or sensibilities, as well as any outcomes of that effort."[33] Cremin suggests that the discipline of education and a history of education must consider the ecology of educational institutions which mediate American culture and character.

The context was then set for a new look at the history of the church's educational efforts. The progressive era had been set apart in Christian education theory and in public school theory, and a new definition of education was now available. Robert Lynn, then a Professor of Religious Education at Union Theological Seminary in New York, stimulated such a new effort with his publication of two popular books: <u>Protestant Strategies in Education</u>, published in 1964, and <u>The Big, Little School: Two Hundred Years of The Sunday School</u>, published in 1971 with Elliott Wright; and with his supervision of many doctoral projects in the history of the church's educational efforts at Union Seminary. Two of his students, Malcolm Warford, now President of Eden Seminary, and John Westerhoff III, now Professor of Pastoral Theology at Duke University Divinity School, have reflected his thesis.

The particular thesis is that the church's educational task has been inappropriately limited to the institution of the Sunday school (or church school). In their minds, the problem with the progressive conception of religious education is that it adhered too easily to John Dewey's school chauvinism which made the school a mini-society and the exclusive agent of education. It thus neglected and interrupted the broader ecology of education true of the nineteenth century. These contemporary historians therefore look back before the "progressive error" to discover the ecology of institutions within which the church's school functioned.

Lynn's analysis becomes paradigmatic for this interpretation. He suggests that in the middle of the nineteenth century a church educational ecology was formed within evangelical Protestant America. This ecology was centered around the social institution of the revival and was extended in the denominational college, the seminary, the public schools (which functioned as Protestant parochial schools), the church mission agencies, reform movements, religious journals, and the Sunday school. It is within this larger ecology that the Sunday school found its place and was effective. To Lynn,

That basic pattern is still in evidence, though often in a feeble and disorderly state. The problems of the contemporary Sunday school are not simply those of one institution, but rather a reflection of a larger systematic confusion within the enterprise as a whole. But wherever the ecology remains intact and the evangelical spirit is strong, there one will discover latter-day reminders of the Sunday school in its hey-day.[34]

Therefore, in present-day evangelical America, represented by the independent Bible churches, where one finds the continuation of this ecology, church educational efforts are still quite strong.[35] The problems of church education are thus attributed to the demise of the pervasive culture of Protestant evangelicalism.

Representatives of this approach suggest that most progressive church educators did not realize the powerful effect of the dissolution of this ecology, and confused the response to it by raising the church school to such a position of importance.[36] The Sunday school, this marginal educational institution, functioned effectively while in the ecology, but set apart from it, its effectiveness was lost.

At this point, Westerhoff states the argument most extremely. He argues that with the dissolution of the ecology, the church school was reduced to the only visible agency of education for the Christian faith. Such a schooling-instructional understanding of education has "victimized" the church and "imprisoned" church educators to its implications.[37] While not using such extreme language, the other historians in this perspective would concur arguing that the self-understanding of educators in the church has been confused because they accept the progressive definition of the church school as an educational agency and do not adequately understand the context within which it was born. The progressive church school is thus seen in significant discontinuity from the Sunday school in the late nineteenth century.

While this interpretation clearly demonstrates that the old cultural ecology fell into disarray at the

13

turn of the century, and the church school therefore had
to function within a new context, it does not suggest
what a new ecology for Christian education might look
like in the present pluralistic culture. It also ex-
aggerates the discontinuities between the nineteenth
century and the twentieth century visions of the church
school. For example, the move to professionalism and
educational effectiveness in the Sunday school can be
traced far back into the nineteenth century. One can
hardly deny that John Vincent, Henry Trumbull, and
Marion Lawrance were professionals who sought to discover the best educational methods. On the other hand,
an awareness of the public ecology for the church's
education was actually born in the work of progressives
like George Albert Coe and William Clayton Bower.[38]

To be sure, many twentieth century educators did
not realize how inextricably tied the Sunday school was
to the broader system of public education even in the
nineteenth century and some did become captured in a
schooling-instructional approach. But this is also
true of many of the earlier nineteenth century educators. They also did not realize the broader ecology
of education. In fact, it appears that nineteenth
century educators stumbled into the effective ecology.
The unity of their culture protected them. Both "new
time" and "old time" were blind to the ecology.

The prevailing contemporary interpretations reflect the thesis of both the liberal progressives and
their neo-orthodox critics when they date the progressive period of religious education as the period of
most significant change and as foundational for the
present.

Emerging Revisionist Interpretations

Continuing to be influenced by the understandings
of the ecology of education developed by Cremin and
used by Lynn, the revisionist historians suggest that
more attention be given to how the nineteenth century
ecology was developed and how it has continued to be
influential. They also draw on revisionist public
education historians who argue that the values and
convictions which constituted the American educational
ecology continue to be used to defend public education
in new situations.[39]

14

Revisionist historians in church education suggest a thesis similar to the public education revisionists. For the church educators, the Sunday school was
forced to deal with questions of the nature of its
school system earlier than the turn of the century,
and the question of how this school functioned within
the matrix of church institutions was a question for
both the nineteenth century and progressive periods.
In fact, it could be argued that the progressives were
more aware of the broader ecology of institutions than
the old-time Sunday school leaders.

The revisionist historians of American public
education are thus having a direct effect on the re-
interpretation of the church's educational work.
They are forcing church educators to look at the for-
mation of the system of public education. For the
public school revisionists, the pattern and system of
urban public education were well in place by the 1880s.
The work of two premier revisionists is illustrative:
Michael B. Katz, Class, Bureaucracy and Schools: The
Illusion of Educational Change in America and David
Tyack, The One Best System: A History of American
Urban Education. Both conclude that an examination of
major urban systems of public education, for example,
Boston, New York, and St. Louis, yields a description
of a centralized bureaucratic form of public schooling
which became paradigmatic for American public educa-
tion.

This system is also found to be in place no later
than the eighth decade of the nineteenth century. The
crucial elements of the paradigm are systemic uniformity of instruction, of structure, and of expecta-
tion enforced by a centralized bureaucracy, graded instruction, promotion based on examinations, unified
courses of study, and a regulated daily schedule. A
premier example of this paradigm is the St. Louis
public schools in the 1870s under the leadership of
William Torrey Harris. Harris believed, "The first
requisite of the school is Order: each pupil must be
taught first and foremost to conform his behavior to a
general standard."[40] Tyack describes how Harris
embodied this principle in St. Louis and transformed
it into a unified system.

They wanted to divide the cities into attendance
districts; calibrate upgraded primary and grammar
schools into distinct classes in which children

15

were segregated according to their academic progress; provide adequate school houses and equipment; train and certify teachers for specific tasks within these graded schools; design a sequential curriculum or program of studies that would be uniform throughout the city; devise examinations which would test the achievement of pupils and serve as a basis for promotion (and often as a basis of evaluating the teacher as well); and provide specialized services such as those given in kindergartens, trade schools, evening schools, and institutions for deviant children who did not fit into the regular classroom. At the top of the system was the superintendent of schools, who, in theory at least, was expected to be the architect and overseer of the entire system, the center of communications and directives for the schools as a whole.[41]

Therefore, within ten years after the Civil War the system of American public instruction was formed and practiced in major urban centers from Boston to Portland. Therefore, as Katz writes, the feeling of educational change in America is an illusion. The progressives merely re-enforced the basic elements of the system.

Parenthetically, great parallels can be drawn between Harris' system in St. Louis and the Sunday school of the same period. Uniformity was also the key issue--uniformity of content all overseen by the superintendent. The decision in 1872 by the Fifth National Sunday School Convention to approve the creation of the Uniform Lesson curriculum is illustrative. This decision gave the superintendent a way to teach teachers, to monitor instruction, and to judge learning.[42] The progressive religious education criticism of the turn of the century is not therefore the creator of a schooling-instructional paradigm, it is rather an attempt to maintain the earlier established alliances of Sunday school and public school.

The revisionist historians of American public education do see shifts between the nineteenth century and twentieth century school; however, these shifts are not in the basis system, structure or convictions, rather they are shifts in how this "system" enforces its structure. It is the movement from a factory

16

understanding of the system to a corporate understanding. As Tyack has demonstrated, the model for the system of the nineteenth century was that of machine or factory.[43] The educational leaders sought to apply the model of industrial growth and effectiveness to insure uniformity; therefore, the words they used were discipline, order, regularity, industry and punctuality. But as the model for economic life shifted from factory to corporation, substantial internal changes resulted, yet the changes sought to strengthen the already established "one best system."[44] Katz states the argument most clearly:

> The structure of American urban education has not changed since late in the nineteenth century; by 1880, the basic features of public education in most major cities were the same as they are today. The absence of those characteristics in some places did not reflect a different pattern of educational development; it represented, rather, a slower rate of urban growth. In time these places, too, acquired the distinctive marks of American urban education. . . . Beyond doubt, there have been educational developments and innovations of first-rate importance since the late nineteenth century. Consider, for instance, the kindergarten, the junior high school, industrial education, testing, the new math. Each has brought about change; but--and this is the important point--it is change within a given structure that itself has not altered.[45]

Church education historians often overlook that there were conflicts in public education with the emergence of the corporate model of rationality and expertise, just as there were conflicts in the leadership of church education. These conflicts though were about shifts within a structure, rather than shifts between structures. The progressive era in religious education advocated changes, but changes within structure.

Describing this public school revisionist interpretation, it is not surprising that the initial steps at revisionist church education history are taken by two persons who were educated respectively by Cremin and Carl Kaestle, the latter who was a great influence on both Tyack and Katz. The initial steps in a revisionist history of church education were represented

17

in a paper by Charles Foster entitled, "Looking from
the Past into the Future of Protestant Church Education," and in a dissertation titled "The Nursery of
the Church: Evangelical Protestant Sunday Schools,
1820-1880," prepared by Anne Mary Boylan for the
faculty of the University of Wisconsin.

In his brief essay, Foster explores this continuity.
He has stated his thesis in the following way:

> Althouth changes in the interpretation of Christian
> life and faith have taken place during the last
> century and a half, I contend that the structure
> of the educational life in American Protestantism
> has been maintained with remarkable consistency,
> and moreover, that this continuity of structure
> has in turn helped perpetuate emphases that edu-
> cational reformers often felt they had replaced
> or altered in their curricular revisions and
> other educational innovations.[46]

By structure, Foster directs his attention to the content of the expectations (that is, self-understanding)
that persons hold for the church's educational ministry.[47] At the pinnacle is the principle of volun-
tarism, that church education is a voluntary association of persons committed to teaching the church's
faith. Therefore, to maintain the church school, this
principle has demanded a simple, efficient structure
which effects clear evidence of performance. Simplicity, efficiency and performance are essential to maintain a person's involvement in a voluntary association.
The uniform lesson material is an example of this structure in action. It defined and limited curriculum to
a short biblical passage, provided an efficient means
of teacher training and instruction, and gave clear
criteria stated in the superintendent's summaries by
which to judge its effectiveness. Secondly, the principle of theological consensus is asserted to maintain
unity in the midst of plurality. The Sunday school has
tended to hold up the common theological denominators,
rather than accentuating the differences. Again the
uniform lesson and the common curricular agreement of
mainline denominations exemplify this trend. Finally.
popular Sunday school expectations are concerned with
personal piety and the moral responsibility of the
individual. While this is particularly revealed in the
unity of evangelical faith, such a concern for personal
experience and appropriation even guides much of the

present church school practice. Foster concludes that until these expectations of the practice of church education are owned and confronted, church education will remain immune to substantial change. He would like to see a church education which transcends the simplicity of structure, encounters theological diversity, and embodies the corporate nature of the Christian community, but he realizes that it is impossible without a new historical understanding.

In much the same way, Anne Boylan seeks to understand the birth of the Sunday school as a church institution. She describes the form which it took at the critical transition from an institution independent of the church to an institution of the church, and she hints at problems which this "new birth" has left for Protestant education.

Sunday schools became agents of religious indoctrination for children of church members, nurturing them in the experiences and beliefs of Protestantism, so that at adulthood they would choose membership in the church. She says that the "Sunday schools frankly assumed the task of training children for membership in a particular sect."[48] Therefore, all questions of educational method, of renewal, and of ministry became subsumed under this purpose of membership or indoctrination. The relationship the Sunday school had with the public school is then a microcosm of decision making within the Sunday school. The relationship was encouraged when it contributed to this basic purpose of forming members, and not encouraged, when it did not.

In her research she has also demonstrated that the development of educational methods for the church's school, the birth of the profession of Sunday school worker and the theology of Christian nurture substantially affected the church's education over twenty-five years earlier than previously assumed.[49] By 1880, the "nursery of the church" was fully functioning. In the church, as well as in the public school, the progressive education movement of the twentieth century is but a culmination and public acceptance of earlier trends.

Foster and Boylan have thus provided clues for a revisionist history of church education. The next task is to examine and describe how continuity was maintained throughout the crucial periods of nineteenth century expansion and progressive "reform," and to highlight the historical alternatives which appeared to challenge this continuity. The problem for the church's school is not simply to reverse a misdirection caused by twentieth century progressives; it is a more complex issue of understanding and confronting shifts within a basic continuity. To paraphrase Katz, the feeling of educational change in the church is an illusion.

Notes

[1] Lawrence Cremin, Traditions of American Education (New York: Basic Books, 1977), pp. 49, 55, 156.

[2] Robert W. Lynn, "The Last of the Great Religious Movements," The Duke Divinity School Review 40 (Fall 1975):160.

[3] The new histories which have been primary to this study are William B. Kennedy, The Shaping of Protestant Education: An Interpretation of the Sunday School and the Development of Protestant Educational Strategy in the United States, 1789-1860 (New York: Association Press, 1966); Robert W. Lynn, Protestant Strategies in Education (New York: Association Press, 1964); Robert W. Lynn and Elliott Wright, The Big Little School: The Sunday Child of American Protestantism (New York: Harper and Row, 1971); Malcolm Warford, The Necessary Illusion: Church Culture and Educational Change (Philadelphia: Pilgrim Press, 1976); Anne M. Boylan, "'The Nursery of the Church:' Evangelical Protestant Sunday Schools, 1820-1880" (Ph.D. dissertation, University of Wisconsin, 1973); and Charles Foster, "Looking from the Past into the Future," Delaware, Ohio, 1977 (photocopied). The last two volumes are representative of the emerging revisionist position.

[4] Henry Clay Trumbull, The Sunday School: Its Origin, Mission, Methods, and Auxiliaries (Philadelphia: John D. Wattles, 1888).

[5] Ibid., p. v.

[6] Ibid., pp. 120-122.

[7] Ibid., pp. 132-133.

[8] Ibid., p. 119.

[9]Ibid., p. vi.

[10]E. Morris Fergusson, Historic Chapters in Christian Education in America: A Brief History of the American Sunday School Movement, and the Rise of the Modern Church School (New York: Fleming H. Revell Co., 1935), p. 5.

[11]Arlo A. Brown, A History of Religious Education in Recent Times (New York: Abingdon Press, 1923); Marianne C. Brown, Sunday-School Movements in America (New York: Fleming H. Revell Co., 1901); Henry Frederick Cope, The Evolution of the Sunday School (Boston: Pilgrim Press, 1911); E. Morris Fergusson, Historic Chapters in Christian Education in America; and Edwin Wilbur Rice, The Sunday-School Movement 1780-1917 and the American Sunday-School Union 1817-1917 (Philadelphia: American Sunday School Union, 1917).

[12]Lawrence A. Cremin, The Wonderful World of Ellwood Patterson Cubberly: An Essay on the Historiography of American Education (New York: Bureau of Publications, Teachers College, Columbia University, 1965). The analysis of a triumphant history of American education is drawn largely from Cremin.

[13]See Burton Bledstein, The Culture of Professionalism: The Middle Class and the Development of Higher Education in America (New York: W. W. Norton & Co., 1976).

[14]Rice, Sunday-School Movement, p. 5.

[15]Many examples could be given. Two are Cope, Evolution of the Sunday School, pp. 85, 107; and Fergusson, Historic Chapters, pp. 100-111.

[16]Cope, Evolution of the Sunday School, p. 100.

[17]Theodore G. Soares, "History of the R.E.A." Religious Education 23 (Convention Issue 1928):621-622.

[18]Fergusson, Historic Chapters, p. 150; Brown, Sunday-School Movements, p. 230; and Cope, Evolution of the Sunday School, p. 85.

[19]To understand the mood during the transition from liberal to neo-orthodox education, see William Clayton Bower, H. Shelton Smith, and Henry P. Van Dusen, "Issues in Religious Education," Religion in Life 7 (Winter 1942-1943):31-52; Adelaide Teague Case, Liberal Christianity and Religious Education: A Study of Objectives in Religious Education (New York: Macmillan Co., 1924); and Hugh Hartshorne, "The Program and Influence of the R.E.A.," Religious Education 49 (March-April 1954):108.

[20]See the following works by Reinhold Niebuhr: Moral Man and Immoral Society (New York: Charles Scribner's Sons, 1941), pp. 120-123; "The Person and the Mind of Man in Modern Education," in Modern Education and Human Values Vol. II (Pittsburgh: University of Pittsburgh Press, 1948), pp. 19-41; and "The Spirit of Life" in National Education Association, Proceedings of 68th Meeting (Washington, D.C.: National Education Association, 1930), pp. 610-618.

[21]Hugh Hartshorne and Earle V. Ehrhardt, Church Schools of Today (New Haven: Yale University Press, 1933); and Hugh Hartshorne and Mark A. May, Studies in the Nature of Character: Studies in Deceit (New York: Macmillan, 1928), p. 359.

[22]Department of Research and Service, The Development of a Curriculum of Religious Education (Chicago: International Council of Religious Education, 1928), p. 12.

[23]H. Shelton Smith, Faith and Nurture (New York: Charles Scribner's Sons, 1941), p. 32.

[24]See for example Reinhold Niebuhr, "Religion and Education," Religious Education 48 (November-December 1953):372-373; and Lynn and Wright, Big Little School, pp. 90-94.

[25]Paul Vieth, ed., The Church and Christian Education (St. Louis: Cooperative Publishing Association, 1947).

[26]The story is told by William Kennedy in his Ph.D. dissertation. William B. Kennedy, "The Genesis and Development of the Christian Faith and Life Series" (Ph.D. dissertation, Yale University, 1957), pp. 98-103.

[27]Ibid., pp. 121, 221, 306-325.

[28]James Smart, "The Why? What? When? of the New Curricu-
lum entitled Christian Faith and Life, A Program for Church and
Home," quoted in Kennedy, "Genessis and Development of the
Christian Faith and Life Series," p. 446.

[29]Bernard Bailyn, Education in the Founding of American
Society (New York: W. W. Norton & Co., 1960); and Cremin,
Wonderful World of Cubberly. The premier American church histor-
ian of the Sunday school, Robert Lynn, trained with Lawrence
Cremin.

[30]Cremin, Wonderful World of Cubberly, p. 43.

[31]Lawrence A. Cremin, Public Education (New York: Basic
Books), pp. 27-53.

[32]Bailyn, Education in the Founding of American Society,
p. 14. Bailyn gave credit to Edward Eggleston's Transit of
Civilization as a forerunner of his position.

[33]Cremin, Public Education, p. 27. This book represents an
overview of Cremin's thesis about American education.

[34]Lynn, "Last of the Religious Movements," p. 153; and
Idem, Protestant Strategies, pp. 22-26. See also Malcolm Warford, The Necessary Illusion, pp. 13-25, 53.

[35]See Elmer Townes, The Ten Largest Sunday Schools and
What Makes Them Grow (Grand Rapids: Baker Book House, 1969),
pp. 113-145.

[36]Lynn and Wright, Big Little School, pp. 77-86; and
Warford, Necessary Illusion, pp. 21-23, 55.

[37]John W. Westerhoff III, Will Our Children Have Faith?
(New York: Seabury Press, 1976), p. 9.

[38]See George Albert Coe, A Social Theory of Religious Edu-
cation (New York: Charles Scribner's Sons, 1927); and William
Clayton Bower, The Curriculum of Religious Education (New York:
Charles Scribner's Sons, 1927).

[39]See Michael Katz, Class, Bureaucracy, and the Schools: The Illusion of Educational Change in America, expanded ed. (New York: Praeger Publishers, 1975); and David Tyack, The One Best System: A History of American Urban Education (Cambridge: Harvard University Press, 1974). In this study, I am relying on the sequence of educational reform established by the revisionists. I am not relying, however, on their radical critique of the progressive era and bureaucracy. For a critique of the revisionists, see Diane Ravitch, The Revisionists Revised: A Critique of the Radical Attack on the Schools (New York: Basic Books, 1978).

[40]Quoted by Tyack, One Best System, p. 43.

[41]Ibid., pp. 43-44.

[42]B. F. Jacob, "The Uniform Lesson Question," in The Fifth National Sunday School Convention (New York: Aug. O Van Lennep, 1872), pp. 84-87.

[43]Tyack, One Best System, p. 42.

[44]Ibid., p. 126. See also Katz, Class, Bureaucracy, and the Schools, pp. 105-146; Raymond E. Callahan, Education and the Cult of Efficiency: A Study of the Social Forces that Have Shaped the Administration of the Public Schools (Chicago: University of Chicago Press, 1962); and Joel Spring, "Education and Progressivism," The History of Education Quarterly 10 (Spring 1970): 53-71.

[45]Katz, Class, Bureaucracy, and the Schools, pp. 105-106.

[46]Foster, "Looking From the Past into the Future," p. 1.

[47]Ibid., pp. 9, 13-16.

[48]Boylan, "Nursery of the Church," p. 317.

[49]Her discussion can be found in chapters 4-6. Ibid., pp. 155-315.

CHAPTER II

FROM MISSION SCHOOL TO
CHURCH'S SCHOOL

Sunday school leaders in the late nineteenth century pointed to the Third National Sunday School Convention held in Philadelphia in 1859 as a watershed in Sunday school history. At this convention, the Sunday school was officially recognized for the first time as a department of the church.[1] While the Sunday school had not fully become an institution of the church by 1859, the convention action did reflect a trend which had been developing in the American Sunday school. From once being an educational institution outside the church, the Sunday school became the educational institution of the church.

The primary resolution of the convention stated the emerging consensus. "Resolved, that we regard the Sunday-school, in connection with the teachings of the Family and the Pulpit, reliable as an agency for bringing the entire youth of our country under the saving influence of the Gospel."[2] This resolution, however, faced heated debate. Several persons wanted to argue that the family and the pulpit were the church's primary educators. Yet, when it was approved, the relationship of the Sunday school to the church was affirmed. The Sunday school was increasingly being recognized as the church's school.

By the time of the Fifth National Sunday School Convention in Indianapolis in 1872, the role of the Sunday school had been further clarified so that the convention historian could declare "the principles of the Sunday-school system were so well understood that all knew what was included in the sphere and work of this agency, and were ready to take up, in their natural order, its various departments."[3] By this time there was no longer any question about the Sunday school being the agency for the church's educational ministry. In these thirteen years the pattern for Protestant education was established.

The Birth of the Sunday School

Great changes had taken place in the Sunday school from the time it was introduced in America after the Revolutionary War until it was clearly defined as the church's school. The first Sunday schools in the United States were modeled after the English counterpart founded by the newspaperman, Robert Raikes. They were philanthropic and educational efforts to train poor children in reading, writing, arithmetic, and morality.

Raikes, a philanthropist interested in prison reform, believed that poverty and ignorance were conditions which bred crime; therefore, if these conditions could be addressed while children were yet innocent and their habits unformed, crime could be reduced. A school on Sunday, the free day of the week, which used the Bible to educate and which used discipline to instill proper habits was proposed as a means for this education for the poor. After a successful experiment which began in 1780 in Sooty Alley, Raikes publically announced his proposal in the Gloucester Journal of 1783. It was accepted as a model by other English philanthropists and some religious leaders such as John Wesley, and Sunday schools were built to extend the benefits of education and biblical teaching to the poor and neglected.[4]

The idea of Sunday schools as instruments for moral and social betterment spread to America. The first Sunday schools in the new world were open to persons who could not otherwise afford to educate themselves and became a means of basic education for the poor as well as the means of preventing a "profanation" of Sunday.[5] They had the support of political, social, and religious leaders. In Philadelphia, for example, Dr. Benjamin Rush was one of the organizers of the First Day Society. He saw the Sunday school as a way of providing the morality and education necessary for the democratic republic.[6] These earliest American Sunday schools, while inspired with religious and humanitarian motives, were almost exclusively founded by public leaders and established outside the church.[7]

Many church leaders questioned the value of the Sunday school. In the revolutionary spirit and with a commitment to freedom of religion, they questioned any British religious innovation, but more importantly they

could not see how the Sunday school could contribute to
the church practices of instruction, catechism, and
preaching. They questioned whether instruction on the
Sabbath was permitted in the Scripture and feared the
great religious authority it gave to religiously untrained laity. Nevertheless, Sunday schools became
religiously inspired schools on Sunday for the education of the poor.

After 1810, Sunday schools expanded with great
rapidity.[8] Several cities including New York, New
Haven, Boston, and Hartford formed Sunday school
unions for the propagation of Sunday schools and
several churches allowed independent Sunday schools to
be held in their facilities. For the next twenty years
most Sunday schools continued to be spread by voluntary
efforts of church leaders and by city unions, independent of the church in terms of educational policy
and financial practices.

The pinnacle of this early development occurred
in 1824 when the American Sunday School Union was
formed with the following purposes:

> to concentrate the efforts of Sabbath school
> societies in the different sections of our country;
> to strengthen the hands of the friends of religious
> instruction on the Lord's Day; to disseminate use-
> ful information, circulate moral and religious
> publications in every part of the land; and to
> endeavor to plant a Sunday school wherever there
> is a population.[9]

It sought to be a missionary for Sunday schools extending education and religious faith into parts of the
country neither touched by school nor church.

The union was a religiously inspired organization,
but it clearly saw its work as outside the church. A
list of doctrinal principles were subscribed to which
were thought to be the essentials of Christian unity
held in common by all evangelical, Protestant denominations. While clergy and denominations were included
in the membership of the society, it was predominantly
lay. Membership was open to all persons who contributed an annual fee to support its work. The society
expressly stated that it was neither a denominational
nor interdenominational group, rather it was a voluntary association of religious persons. In its make-up

27

it mirrored the constituency of the Sunday school movement.

The Sunday School Union also distinguished its task from that already being done by the family, the church, and the state. Filling the gaps left by the others was its stated purpose. Parents were encouraged to lead children into moral character, but where this was not true the society proposed to provide family religious instruction. The society tried not to infringe upon the tasks of the church, but to cultivate an area for the church's ministry. Also they did not propose to infringe upon the state, but to stimulate it to provide free schools. The society saw its task as providing educational ideas, literature and supplies, extending teacher education throughout the country, and facilitating the spread of Sunday schools.[10]

A mission statement of the society written in 1828 is a clear statement of how most Sunday schools defined their task.

The Sunday school: an institution "eminently adapted to promote the intellectual and moral culture of the nation, to perpetuate our republican and religious institutions, and to reconcile eminent national prosperity with moral purity and future blessedness."[11]

The Sunday school was an institution for moral and religious education.

While the earliest Sunday schools were located in the large cities of the Northeast and Mid-Atlantic and attended primarily to the needs of the poor, in the mid-1920s the Sunday school extended its mission to those without education and churches in the rural and frontier areas of America. The first official Sunday school missionaries were sent out by the Sunday and Adult School Union, an outgrowth of Philadelphia's First-Day Society. Initial efforts were made to distribute literature throughout the frontier as well as extend Sunday schools to Indians and to Blacks. As a result of these efforts thirteen Indian Sunday schools, several schools for Blacks, and sixty-one other Sunday schools were formed. The movement to extend education and religious education to the frontier was initiated.[12]

28

The primary effort at frontier expansion was initiated by the American Sunday School Union in 1829. In its Mississippi Valley Enterprise an attempt was made to establish by 1832 a Sunday school in every place where it was practicable in that area. This effort was indeed monumental requiring nearly $90,000 for the two years. It received the support of many prominent clergy and political leaders who saw it as an effort to extend Christian civilization into the unstable western territories. Judged as a great success, this effort was particularly credited with the initiation of the free public school system in the Middle West as well as with saving souls and extending Christian character.[13] A southern and a world-wide strategy to found Sunday schools followed.

During this early period the Sunday school could best be described as an effort supported by the voluntary contributions of Protestants, sometimes with the support of their churches, to extend religion among the poor and the isolated. The Sunday school was a philanthropic and missionary effort.

From Mission School to Church's School

From the mid-1820s until the Civil War, it appears that the Sunday school existed with two objectives. One objective is described by William Alcott, a New England Congregationalist, who argued that the "best children of our best and most pious families" attend Sunday school; while the other is described by James Alexander, a Presbyterian, who called Sunday schools "the best means yet devised for the rapid and successful instruction and salvation of the multitudes who are perishing for lack of knowledge."[14] This dual purpose continued in the minds of some proponents until the 1860s. Theodore Runyon in his address of welcome to the Fourth National Sunday School Convention, reflected both shapes of the Sunday school. On the one hand he applauded the Sunday school for being the "leaven of society," reaching all classes and spreading the practice of virtue on which political institutions reside; on the other hand, he applauded it as the church's institution which makes good Christians.[15]

During these years the Sunday school was both a mission school for the poor and a means of religious instruction for the faithful. However, it was only

29

from the perspective of the 1860s that these two usages
could be clearly distinguished, for the Sunday school
was being defined as the latter, a church institution,
and the mission school became a special term used for
a particular institution with a particular function of
ministering to the poor in the city and on the frontier.
The purpose upon which the Sunday school was founded
was being altered.

The Mission School

The story of the development of the mission school
demonstrates the changes that were taking place in the
Sunday school. By the 1850s the phrase "mission" began to refer to one form of the Sunday school outreach.
Its task was distinguished from the common schools,
which by 1850 were thought to attend to the secular
education of children, and from the church's Sunday
school for church members' children. Therefore, the
mission school was seen as exclusively a religious
education and service enterprise for the poor.

While it claimed a collegial relationship with the
common school in molding the national character, it was
primarily defined as a mission enterprise which evan-
gelized the poor, particularly ethnic groups, by providing instruction in religion, recreation, and social
service.[16] Therefore, its mission was much more
religious and evangelistic than educational, and its
program was usually funded and administered by a local
church.[17]

It was also distinguished from the church's Sunday
school. It was an adjunct for the unchurched and the
poor. Two model examples are the Bethel Mission of
Plymouth Church in Brooklyn and the Railroad Mission
of First Presbyterian Church in Chicago. Bethel Mission provided Sunday evening services, weekly recreation and entertainment events, and reading rooms for
mechanics and boys, as well as an educational program.[18]
Henry Ward Beecher, the pastor of Plymouth Church,
believed these schools should be like real homes where
the poor could find escape from the city and nourish-
ment into a new way of life.[19] In the same way, the
Railroad Mission provided food, fuel and clothing for
the needy as well as a youth group and children's
classes. The purpose of the mission school was stated

clearly by those at First Church as "the rescue and sanctification of souls."[20]

Beginning in the 1850s and 1860s many Sunday school leaders had to plead with church leaders to support the mission schools and not to forget the poor. They feared that in the new enthusiasm in the church for church Sunday schools the original mission purpose of the Sunday school would be forgotten. The Fourth National Sunday School Convention scheduled a major symposium to promote mission schools and The Sunday School Teacher printed a series of articles outlining the need for and practice of mission schools.[21] Henry Ward Beecher stated the case forcefully when he declared:

> Through mission schools will be reached thousands that will not be reached by the Church alone. . . . There is where you have to get them, and prepare them, and bring them instrumentally into the Church of Christ. . . . I believe in bringing the Church to bear upon the world; and here is the way we Protestant _must_ bring the Church to bear upon the world; and upon the whole country, and utilize our men and women in such a way that the poor shall have the Gospel preached to them, the unfortunate shall be relieved, and the great moral sores in our cities shall be healed.[22]

The forceful advocacy of the mission school and the fear that its message would be lost signaled the change which was taking place in the Sunday school. The Sunday school itself was no longer the free school for the poor, independent of the church. It was the instructional program of the church attending primarily to church members.

The Church's School

Since the 1820s, the Sunday school had slowly become the church's school. A gradual acceptance of the Sunday school by the church and the growth of the common school movement are the two causes of the shift in the function of the Sunday school.

Several church leaders saw that it could provide religious instruction and be an entry point into the life of the church for the children of church members.

One story told in the Sunday schools histories is
how the Reverend Lyman Beecher sent his own children
and induced many of the leaders of his congregation to
send their children to a Sunday school to demonstrate
that it was not only for the poor.[23] The Sunday and
Adult School Union also advocated in the 1920s the
expansion of the Sunday school to the upper classes,
for they believed that its instruction was as useful
to the rich and the believers as to the poor and the
ignorant. They stated that:

> Your board has witnessed with regret the preva-
> lence of an erroneous sentiment respecting the
> principles of Sunday-schools. It is this--that
> they are intended only for the poor. This has
> arisen from the improper application of the prin-
> ciples of gratuitous instruction. These schools
> are intended as much for the affluent as the
> indigent. The great object is religious instruc-
> tion; it is, indeed given without money and with-
> out price--is it, therefore, of no value to those
> who have the means and who, if it were venible,
> would secure it by purchase?[24]

Note here the emphasis on religious instruction as primary aim of the Sunday school. Several churches in the
late 1820s transformed their Sunday schools. Park
Street Church in Boston is an example. Its Sunday
school, which had been founded in 1817 as a mission for
the poor, became in 1829 a school for the church.[25]

Several denominations both organized Sunday schools
on mission frontiers and encouraged churches to extend
the Sunday school to their members.[26] The Methodist
Episcopal Church is the best example. By 1824, the
church's General Conference had encouraged all traveling
preachers to establish Sunday schools. By 1827, a
special Sunday-School Union was established for Methodists to continue the development of schools of local
churches. No other denomination so early developed such
an official organization for the promotion of the Sunday school, but by the 1860s almost all denominations
had encouraged the development of the Sunday school as
a department of the church and several joined in the
effort to publish Sunday school texts.[27]

In fact, the rush to establish denominational control over the Sunday school was so extensive that it is
said to have inaugurated a period in the history of

32

Sunday school curriculum called the "Babel period."[28]
With so many competing publishers and texts, the unity
of the voice of the American Sunday School Union had
given way in the 1850s to the many voices.

By the 1850s, most congregations had made the
Sunday school a part of their ministry to church
families. Churches perceived that the Sunday school
had much to offer it. As Anne Boylan has noted, much
of the early resistance to the Sunday school was because of a feeling ". . . that such schools somehow
usurped the traditional roles of parents and ministers."[29] In the minds of Sunday school advocates
these criticisms needed to be overcome.

The idea was accepted that the parental responsibility for religious education was enhanced by the
ministries of the church and the school. Here again
the Beecher family is an example. Catherine Beecher,
the daughter of Lyman Beecher, included this idea in
her 1864 book on the religious training of children
entitled Religious Training of Children in the School,
the Family and the Church. She argued that "Religious
training . . . embraces all modes of influencing a
child to obey the laws of God."[30] Therefore, all these
forces should be coordinated to teach the child the
Christian life and protect his or her fate in eternity.
Another Sunday school leader, Henry Clay Trumbull, concluded that the Sunday school not only complemented
family instruction, but stimulated it. He argued that,
"The Family is, in the providence of God, incomplete,
hence insufficient for the religious training of the
young."[31] For him, this notion was fully demonstrated
in the evidence from England, Ireland, Scotland, Wales,
and America that household religion had been stimulated
by the Sunday school.

The pastoral problem was also addressed when Sunday schools moved into the church and became part of
the church's ministry, rather than an external lay-led
endeavor. Laity were still primary, but pastors could
now influence the instructional and the policy decisions.
In the Fourth National Sunday School Convention in
1869, a special section on "Ministers and Pastors" was
initiated. It advocated that the pastor by office was
head of the Sunday school.[32] This statement represents
a significant shift of emphasis from what was represented by earlier Sunday school leaders. The authority
of the pastor was recognized. In fact, by the 1870s

and 1880s, some leaders pleaded with pastors to be more involved in the workings of their Sunday schools. In addition, they advocated that ministry training should include attention to the Sunday school and Sunday school procedures.[33]

However, a primary reason for the inclusion of the Sunday school in the church's ministry was the recognition that the Sunday school was contributing both children and adult members to the church. By 1880, denominational leaders had statistics that showed that 80 percent of all new members came into the church through the Sunday school.[34] These statistics had been recognized intuitively much earlier; in the 1850s many denominational leaders were comfortable in calling the Sunday school the "nursery of the church." For example, an 1850 history of Massachusetts Sunday schools concluded,

> It is felt, if there is any good reason for each denomination to have its distinctive churches, there is an equally good reason for having its distinct Sabbath school operations. This institution is the nursery of the church. To its members every church is looking for her future enlargement. But if the children are left untaught, in regard to all those truths which are distinctive, what security has she that another will not gather the harvest from the seed which she has herself sown and nurtured? If the truths and principles that are distinctive to any given denomination, are not of enough importance to have them taught to the young--to those to whom the churches of the denomination are to be replenished and perpetuated--then those truths and principles are not of sufficient importance to justify the existence of that denomination.[35]

It was agreed that the Sunday school could exist under church control and enhance the ministry and the membership of the church. Its existence in two forms was encouraged, church's school and mission school, but both were to be, as a Sunday school missionary, John McCullagh, stated, ". . . a grand church-extension scheme."[36]

The Sunday School and the Public School

This redefinition of the Sunday school was also encouraged by developments in the public school movement. With the development of the public school, the original form of the Sunday school had seemed no longer needed. The American system of education consisting of private academies, apprentice training, charity schools, Sunday school, and some publicly-funded schools had given way by 1860 to a system of public instruction. Only in remote places did church-sponsored free schools continue to be needed.

An influential American educator and historian of American education, Henry Barnard, wrote in 1865 of this relationship in the influential American Journal of Education.

Religious instruction has been withdrawn from the common school and intrusted wholly to the home and the church; and as "the Evangelist of the district school," the Sunday-school has arisen, not indeed to interrupt or displace parental and pastoral culture but to supply their unavoidable deficiencies and to act where they can not.[37]

Barnard believed that the common school and the Sunday school had grown to be partners in a symbiotic relationship where innovations in one were shared with the other and where together the whole person was educated--in mind, body, and morality by the common school, and in spirit and religion by the Sunday school.

The initial relationship of church leaders to the common school movement had been mixed, some thinking it was a significant innovation which their work in the Sunday school had effected, and others fearing that the common school would usurp responsibilities of home and church. Yet, the public school movement expanded rapidly through the 1840s, 1850s, and 1860s. It was seen as a great social tool for educating the population for democracy and for incorporating the vast numbers of American immigrants into American culture. Protestants particularly came to support it because their concerns were answered by common school leaders who limited the public schools to cultural and moral educational tasks and openly accepted the religious and doctrinal education tasks of the church. Protestants also began to see Catholic immigration as more of

35

a threat than a secular common school which was to teach American culture. The public school in fact was an evangelical Protestant parochial school.[38]

Just such a separation of functions seems intimated in the early records of the American Sunday School Union where the establishment of common schools was encouraged and a declaration was made that even when such education was developed that the Sunday school would still have a religious education task ". . . to make the young thoroughly acquainted with the Word of God."[39] A partnership was effected between public and common school.

> The two were seen together as great leveling institutions of society. Each contributed to the other. . . . By teaching morality and the Bible, the day school served, in Horace Mann's words, as a "powerful auxiliary" to religious education. Because of the instruction given in Sunday school, the public school needed to provide only elementary religious teaching.[40]

By 1872 Sunday school leaders could claim that the change in the definition of the Sunday school had been completed. Its purpose, its form, and its scope were clear to all parties. Denominational and interdenominational groups cooperated in the development of this institution and the great heyday of the Sunday school was ready to begin. The Sunday school had become the nursery of the church. As Anne Boylan so clearly states:

> Over the course of about fifty years 1820-1870, the definition of a Sunday school had undergone a complete reversal. Began as schools exclusively for the religious education of non-churchgoers' children, they became institutions almost exclusively for the children of the church. In the process of reversal, schools which began as missionary institutions often found themselves, ten or twenty years later, organizing a mission or branch school to accommodate the children for whom the school was originally gathered. Designed as institutions for reaching the unchurched, Sunday schools became a substitute for evangelization, eliminating the churches' need to bring in new members through conversion.[41]

36

The Nursery of the Church

The conception of the Sunday school as the nursery of the church was foundational for the future theory and practice of the Sunday school. The story of the Sunday school from the Civil War to the present is an expansion of this notion. The Sunday school, which once existed outside the church, was now assimilated into the church, but questions of the theological rigor, the educational style, and the relationship to other church agencies which were raised about it continue into our day. It is important to look at the shape of this new Sunday school that had emerged in terms of its purpose, form, and scope.

Purpose

The aim of the new Sunday school was to evangelize and nurture persons into Christianity and to assist persons to grow in understanding and living the faith. This agenda for the Sunday school and its success were articulated by Henry Clay Trumbull who in 1888 wrote

> . . . the Sunday-school has become the prime church agency for pioneer evangelizing, for Bible teaching, and for the religious instruction and care of children, in every denomination of Protestant Christians in America. . . . From an aggregate membership of a few hundred at the beginning of the century, it has come to include, within the evangelical Protestant bodies alone, from eight to ten millions or nearly one-fifth of the entire population of the United States.[42]

The Sunday school was defined as an institution of the church and thus totally dependent on the church for support and policy.[43] Special attention was given in interdenominational efforts to guard the role of the church in Sunday school leadership. Even the American Sunday School Union, which had been seen by many to establish schools in competition to the church, emphasized how its work was to support the church and to lead children into local churches.[44] The best signal of church involvement, however, is the increase in denominational Sunday school work. The Methodists were followed in giving a formal role to the Sunday school by the Congregationalists, Baptists, Lutherans, Unitarians, and Presbyterians.

37

The Sunday school was also defined as more religious than educational. "Otherwise it has no right to its central possession of the Lord's day and the Lord's house," declared one seminary professor of the period.[45] For the first time, <u>Christian</u> education was specifically stated as its purpose.[46] Sunday school and church officials committed themselves to the building of the spiritual nature of the child. To accomplish this agenda required the conversion of the child, the formation of Christian character, and the teaching of Christian or biblical knowledge.[47]

To form a Christian culture or Christian character are expressions that seem to stand out in the writings of the period. While conversion was defined as the first and most important event, and Biblical knowledge was seen as essential to conversion and growth, the inculcation of Christian character was thought to be the pinnacle of the process. Through this means it was hoped that the child could avoid temptation; acquire the traits of self-denial, liberality, virtue, industry, temperance, etc.; and participate in the building of a Christian culture.

By the 1880s, increased attention was given to extending these purposes of conversion, formation, and knowledge to adults. The word "nursery" which had earlier denoted that the Sunday school was the children's ministry of the church came to mean that the Sunday school was a primary entry point into the life and mission of the church.[48] The reasoning was that if it was so effective in teaching children to fulfill Christian responsibilities, it could help adults be more mature Christian persons.

The formation of Christian character became the premier task for the Sunday school. The Sunday school was judged on how effective it was in inculcating proper behavior. Knowledge and even conversion (for it demanded fruits) were seen as means to the end, Christian character. One educator summarized the aim in the phrase "instruction in righteousness."[49] It is precisely this concern for behavior which many modern Christian education critics see as the legacy of the Sunday school. The Sunday school seems to have lacked a serious engagement with theology throughout its history. Theological reflection was often so overshadowed that superficial cultural notions of appropriate behavior were substituted for Christian definitions of reality.[50] To a great extent this criticism can be demonstrated through the history of the Sunday school, for many persons looked uncritically to it to socialize children into polite manners. One list of Sunday school rules includes such things as

> I MUST ALWAYS BE STILL
> I must take good care of by book
> I must not lean on the next boy
> I must walk softly in the School.[51]

In addition, it was seen by many as a way to protect American culture from the influx of immigration. The Rev. Z. M. Humphrey echoed the concerns of many Sunday school and political leaders when he argued that the Sunday school helped in ". . . developing a spirit of patriotism."[52] It took the immigrants who had a tendency to "Romanism," and blended them into the national unity. "The prejudices of race are stubborn and powerful. They can be softened and subdued most readily by the power of common ideas, and by habits of social intercourse."[53] Such was the task of the Sunday school-- taming the "wild democrat of the streets" and preparing him for citizenship and self-government through the teaching of "pure and spiritual Christianity."[54] Concerns for character building were primary in the church Sunday schools as well as their subordinates, the mission Sunday schools.

Form

A consistent plea in Sunday school literature from 1860 was for improvement in the system of Sunday school instruction. In response, church educators looked to the partner of the Sunday school, the public school, as the institution which could provide this improvement. J. M. Gregory expressed this response by listing the particular innovations which the Sunday school had to address: the providing of more comfortable classrooms, the developing of a better system of classifying and grading pupils, the securing of higher quality and trained teachers, and the preparing of more adequate methods of instruction.[55]

Gregory's argument was persuasive because he held, as did most others, the belief that the Sunday school was a segment of the public school movement.

The Sunday School is not an isolated and eccentric
movement of human benevolence. . . . It is but a
part--the religious part--of that great movement
of the age which has organized the common school
systems of the world, and is everywhere marshaling
the forces of civilized peoples and government for
the education of the rising generations. And as
the common, public schools are steadily mounting
an ever advancing wave of popular regard, to
greater efficiency and strength, to better methods
and nobler work; so must the Sunday school, born
of the great fundamental ideas and borne onward by
the same growing power of popular opinion, advance
to new and riper forms of work and to a new and
richer fruitage.[56]

Therefore, teaching became the primary metaphor and day
school methods became the primary form used by the
Sunday school to fulfill its ends. While several Sunday school leaders feared the wholesale acceptance of
day school methods, most argued that these methods improved the system of religious instruction as long as
they were used to enhance the spiritual nature of the
child.[57] Typical was Howard Crosby, who wrote ". . .
the philosophy of teaching in the Sabbath-school is the
philosophy of teaching generally," as was Joseph Alden
when he argued that the distinction some were making
between religious and secular education was unsound.[58]
In fact, by 1873 one school, Cincinnati Wesleyan College
for Young Women, taught a course of instruction for
Sunday school teachers out of its teacher training program.[59]

The four issues which Gregory had listed for the
Sunday school to confront to enhance its educational
system were addressed in the 1860s and 1870s, that is
Sunday school buildings, classification, teacher
training, and methods of instruction. These issues
have continued for Sunday school practice.

In terms of buildings, the Sunday school literature
of the 1860s and 1870s is filled with criticism of the
adapted facilities which housed most Sunday schools.
Attention was particularly given to the need for more
lighting, more ventilation, more comfortable furniture,
and more instructional aids. The ideal Sunday school
building was thought to have been erected in the
Methodist Episcopal Church of Akron, Ohio in the late
1850s.[60] The Akron plan thus became the model of

40

excellence. It consisted of a central lecture room which could be overseen by the Sunday school superintendent and partitioned smaller rooms where individual classes could meet. Being a truly multipurpose model, the lecture room could double in a smaller church as church sanctuary and the superintendent's desk as the pulpit. The facility included office space, church library, and kitchen. It was built to include all of the necessities for supervised, graded instruction which good education demanded.

The superintendent could lead the opening exercises and initiate the lesson from the central desk. The students could then partition their classes, with minimal disruption, for class instruction and then again with little effort gather for the closing exercises. Space to store instructional supplies as well as preparation space for teachers was provided.

The classification of pupils was an issue which continued for much longer before it was finally resolved. As early as the middle of the 1860s, publications began to appear which advocated that graded departments were the most efficient means of instruction. One author suggested that the Sunday school be divided into departments of primary (those under 8 years old), intermediate (8-12 years old), junior (12-15 years old), and senior (those over 15).[61] At this time grading merely meant the dividing of pupils into age categories; it did not mean providing different content for each age level. It was much later, at the turn of the century, that grading came to mean both age-graded classes, and curriculum like the public school. Between 1890 and 1910, there was much controversy before the more specialized definition was accepted.[62]

However, it did not take long for a system of dividing pupils into age-graded classes, all using the same lesson, to become accepted Sunday school practice. By 1872, the uniform lesson curriculum was initiated. It was intended to provide one lesson for graded classes in Sunday schools throughout the world.[63] By 1878, the International Sunday School Convention was even advocating supplemental lessons to enhance the age-grade classifications.[64]

Improving the quality of teachers had been seen for a long time as the key ingredient in improving the effectiveness of Sunday school instruction. In the

late 1850s John Vincent, the Methodist Sunday school
leader, introduced the model of "normal classes" for
Sunday school teachers.[65] The Sunday school normal
institute quickly became a practice throughout the
Sunday school world.

During the Fourth National Sunday School Convention, a resolution was passed to support the founding
of an International Training College, following the
pattern of the secular normal schools "to teach teachers
to teach." These colleges were to concentrate on the
idea and method of teaching, the principles of teaching
Scripture, and the organization of the Sunday school.[66]
State conventions and teachers' institutes were encouraged by the International Sunday School Convention,
and Sunday school periodicals expanded their attention
to methods of teaching. A new journal was founded in
1875 for the express purpose of teaching teachers, The
Normal Class.[67]

Several designs for teacher training were published.
One of the most extensive was the design used at Bald-
win University in Berea, Ohio. Lectures were given on
the following themes:

1. "The Family, the Pulpit, the Social Meetings
   of the Church and the Sunday-School; their
   relation, and how they may be rendered
   mutually helpful"
2. Duties of Teachers
3. "How to win and retain attention of Scholars"
4. Teaching
5. Church History
6. "Jesus as Model Teacher"
7. "Holy Ghost as Teacher."[68]

While this design was not duplicated everywhere, significant and increasing attention was given to upgrading teacher qualifications through teacher instruction. Yet, for all the emphasis on improving the
quality of teachers, the central aim of the Sunday
school was not forgotten. The spiritual preparation
of the teacher was thought to be as important as the
intellectual preparation. The teacher was not only to
be a conveyer of knowledge, but to invoke spiritual
growth in the pupil.[69]

Finally, the Sunday school struggled to improve
its method of teaching. Between 1869 and 1872, there

was significant controversy about the idea of uniform lesson instruction, advocated most forcefully by B. F. Jacobs, a Baptist Sunday school leader from Chicago. The plan for uniform instruction consisted of the development of a series of Bible lessons which would become an outline for national instructional content for Sunday school instruction. Jacobs foresaw a dream where every Sunday school in the world would study one lesson.[70] The plan was advocated as improving Sunday school instruction because teachers could prepare together, superintendents could oversee instruction, parents and children could discuss common learnings in the Sunday school program, and a higher quality of instructional material could be prepared on a national basis.

A form of uniform lesson system had already been in publication since the 1850s. By the late 1860s, the most popular Sunday school magazine, The Sunday School Teacher, provided a uniform series of lessons and a method of instruction which was used in many Sunday schools.[71] The International Sunday School Convention then took the lead in 1872 with the approval of a plan to develop a national model for a uniform lesson series.[72] Within the next ten years, most Protestant denominations had followed suit and were providing lessons based on the uniform lesson plan.[73] One model is the Berean Series edited for the Methodists by John Vincent. The series, based on the International Bible passages, contained leaflets for children and instructional aids for teachers and superintendents.

The Sunday school thus expanded its form relating to developments in the public schools. Issues of architecture, grading, qualified teachers, and improved methods began to be addressed. While the influence was really two-way through the 1880s, the Sunday school increasingly had to respond to issues of educational style and content raised by the public schools. By the late 1800s, the public school seemed so to outdistance its Sunday school counterpart that there was an increased move to improve the quality of Sunday school practice. The impetus for this improvement in fact fueled much of the energy of progressive religious education.

As with the question of purpose, the new form was not without its critics. Again the issues raised form the backdrop for issues in the present day. R. G.

43

Pardee was not alone when he declared, "The mass of Sunday-schools are modelled too much after the task-lessons and strict discipline of day-schools."[74] Others continually reminded Sunday school educational reformers that the spiritual influence of the Sunday school, not knowledge, was the appropriate test of quality in the Sunday school.

Scope

The relationship of the Sunday school to the total ministry of the church was also an issue. When the Sunday school moved into the church, attention had to be given to the relationship of this program to cate-chizing, confirmation classes, worship, family instruc-tion, adult and youth study groups, and parochial schools.[75] The theory of most Sunday school leaders was that these various educational programs of the church could be unified.

The Fifth National Sunday School Convention sought to address the issue of unity. Taking as its theme the sowing of the seed, the convention studied how the seed, the word of God, was sown, by whom and in what fields. The Sunday school was defined as one means of sowing the seed. Therefore, the position advocated at the convention was that sharing the good news was pri-mary; therefore, all instrumentalities of the church worked together for this purpose.[76] Special sessions were held on how the sowing was accomplished in the fields of the family, the Sunday school and the sanc-tuary. A grand design for evangelism and nurture that consisted of these three elements was proposed. The enthusiastic acceptance of this notion is represented in the summary comments made by H. Thane Miller.

> Let us form a new resolve before God Almighty, here tonight, that in our families as well as in the Sunday-school, and in the sanctuary, and in our every hour's experience, we will hear these dear children upon our hearts. Oh how different you will then transact your business! How dif-ferent you will discharge your duties at hand![77]

Increased efforts were given to relating Sunday school, family and pulpit. One of the reasons the uniform lesson curriculum was approved was its apparent solution to the problem of relating agencies of

44

education and ministry. The dream was that all of the agencies of the church could jointly proclaim the same passage of Scripture, worship the God it reflected, and engage in service from it. The Reverend Alfred Taylor of New York stated this dream. "God hasten the time when the pulpit, the pew, the choir, the Sunday-school teacher, and the superintendent will harmoniously work on the same passage of Scripture."[78] The pastor's role in the Sunday school was also advocated because of this dream of unity. It was believed that since the pastor saw the total picture, he was the key person to oversee how ministries of the church interacted with each other.[79] He could lead the church in studying the Scripture. That study could be reenforced in family study and worship, congregational worship, and the Sunday school.

However, despite the theory of unity which embraced the Sunday school, the unity was actually achieved only in rare instances. Many pastors accepted the Sunday school for its contribution to the membership of the church, but as today they left the Sunday school primarily in the hands of the laity. Some churches would also refuse to supplement the budget of the Sunday school when it was needed. While the Sunday school became part of the church, in many ways it remained a separate institution within the church.

Realizing the tensions, several Sunday school leaders sought to convince both church and Sunday school advocates that they needed each other. One Connecticut minister, L. T. Chamberlain, commented that the Sunday School was the "brightest gem" in the church's "crown of glory."[80] He argued that while there had been tension that Sunday school work had to be related to other agencies for their mutual effectiveness. The home, the church, and the minister were the areas of his focus. The highest efficiency would not be achieved, he argued, until a mutual relationship existed. For example, families need instruction and the school and the church need their support. Also, while the Sunday school needed the pastor's leadership, it provided an important source of influence for the pastor. The Sunday school leaders sought a unity in the educational aspects of the congregation. In the late nineteenth century while such a unity was desired, there was great difficulty in achieving it. The relationship of the educational ministry to the congregation's wider ministry continues today as a problem.

45

In the late nineteenth century a cultural unity did support the Sunday school and extended its scope. As Robert Lynn has convincingly demonstrated, the Sunday school existed within a wider ecology of education consisting of revival, public schools, church agencies, reform movements, and religious press.[81] Sunday school leaders were aware of this supportive context and sought to strengthen the unity it represented. While praising the importance of their own institution, they lent support to efforts to extend public schooling and provided lessons on reform movements, particularly temperance. Not only did they want to unite the Sunday school to the church, but they felt they were part of an effort which was uniting the United States into one people-- a Christian people.[82]

The Sunday school was not to be a peripheral agency alongside the church, public school, or reform efforts. It was to be a central pin in a wider effort at Christianization and human betterment.

By 1870, the Sunday school had become unquestionably the nursery of the church. From its beginnings as a religiously-inspired mission outside the church to educate the poor and the isolated, it had moved into the church as the church's primary vehicle of Christian education. Its aim was to evangelize and nurture children. (This was to be expanded to adults by the 1880s). Its form was the emerging school practice. Its scope was to include all the educational aspects of the church's life. This aim, form, and scope have continued into the present and provide Christian education with important questions. The quality of the church's theological education, its understanding of the nature of the church and the community of faith, and the shape of its ministry can be traced in part to this early form established for its educational ministry.

Notes

[1] Henry Clay Trumbull, "Historical Introduction," in The Fifth National Sunday-School Convention (New York: Aug. O Van Lennep, 1872), p. 16.

[2] Ibid.

[3] Ibid., p. 22.

[4]This story is told in many Sunday school histories. See Edwin Wilbur Rice, The Sunday School Movement 1780-1917 and the American Sunday-School Union 1817-1917 (Philadelphia: American Sunday-School Union, 1917), pp. 13-17.

[5]See in addition to Rice, Anne M. Boylan, "'The Nursery of the Church': Evangelical Protestant Sunday Schools, 1820-1860" (Ph.D. dissertation, University of Wisconsin, 1973), pp. 5-9. The role of the Sunday school in the American educational system is told in most histories of education. See for example Robert L. Church, Education in the United States: An Interpretive History (New York: Free Press, 1976), p. 78; and Carl F. Kaestle, The Evolution of an Urban School System: New York, 1750-1850 (Cambridge: Harvard University Press, 1973), pp. 120-126. Many of the following details are drawn from these sources.

[6]Frank Glenn Lankard, A History of The American Sunday School Curriculum (New York: Abingdon Press, 1927), p. 57.

[7]Boylan, "Nursery of the Church," pp. 73-74; and Rice, Sunday School Movement, pp. 43-44.

[8]Henry Clay Trumbull, "Relation of Sunday-School Work to Home Instruction," in The Third [Fourth] National Sunday-School Convention of the United States, 1869 (Philadelphia: J. C. Garrigues & Co., 1869), p. 51. In 1869 when the convention was held, the planners thought that they were planning the Third National Convention. After the 1872 publication of Trumbull's history of the convention system, it was renumbered to be number four; therefore, any footnote reference to the book, The Third National Sunday School Convention, will really indicate this fourth convention held in 1869.

[9]Rice, Sunday School Movement, p. 79.

[10]Ibid., pp. 80-87.

[11]Quoted by Robert W. Lynn and Elliott Wright, The Big Little School: The Sunday Child of American Protestantism (New York: Harper & Row, 1971), p. 1.

[12]Rice, Sunday School Movement, pp. 67-69.

[13]Ibid., pp. 196-201.

[14] Boylan, "The Nursery of the Church," p. 64. Boylan's study is a very helpful description of the transition from Sunday school as mission school to church's school.

[15] Theodore Runyon, "The Address of Welcome," in The Third National Sunday-School Convention, pp. 7-9.

[16] An example of this attitude is reflected in Z. M. Humphrey, "The National Importance of the Mission Sunday School," The Sunday School Teacher 1 (June 1866):161.

[17] See John Vincent, "Editor's Reply," Sunday School Journal for Teachers and Young People 3 (May 1871):106; and Henry Ward Beecher, "The Mission Work of the Sunday School," in The Third National Sunday-School Convention, p. 69. Hereafter in references to the Sunday School Journal for Teachers and Young People, it will be noted as Sunday School Journal.

[18] "The Bethel Mission of Plymouth Church, Brooklyn, N.Y." The National Sunday School Teacher 4 (February 1869):43-44.

[19] Beecher, "The Mission Work of the Sunday-School," p. 75.

[20] Z. M. Humphrey, "The Mission Sunday School Work of the First Presbyterian Church, Chicago," The Sunday School Teacher 2 (March 1867):72.

[21] See The Third National Sunday School Convention, pp. 69-91. The Sunday School Teacher 2 (March 1867):67-72; (October 1867):294-298; 3 (April 1868):111-112; and The National Sunday School Teacher 4 (February 1869):43-44.

[22] Beecher, "The Mission Work of the Sunday-School," pp. 73, 76, 77.

[23] See Marianna C. Brown, Sunday-School Movements in America (New York: Fleming H. Eevell Co., 1901), p. 24.

[24] Rice, Sunday School Movement, p. 68.

[25] Boylan, "The Nursery of the Church," p. 62.

[26] Brown, Sunday-School Movement, pp. 131-152.

[27]William Bean Kennedy, The Shaping of Protestant Education: An Interpretation of the Sunday School and the Development of Protestant Educational Strategy in the United States, 1789-1860 (New York: Association Press, 1966), p. 31.

[28]Lankard, The American Sunday School Curriculum, pp. 175-200.

[29]Boylan, "Nursery of the Church," p. 73. See also p. 76.

[30]Catherine E. Beecher, Religious Training of Children in the School, the Family and the Church (New York: Harper and Bros., 1864), p. 10. For a survey of the American development of religious ideas about children, see Peter Gregg Slater, Children in the New England Mind: In Death and in Life (Hamden, Conn.: Archon Books, 1977).

[31]Trumbull, "Relation of the Sunday-School Work to Home Instruction," pp. 46-47.

[32]George Z. Peltz, "Ministers and Pastors," in The Third National Sunday-School Convention, p. 92.

[33]Henry Clay Trumbull, The Sunday-School: Its Origin, Mission, Methods, and Auxiliaries (Philadelphia: John D. Wattles, 1888), p. vii. See also W. F. Crafts, "The Pastor and the Sunday-School" Sunday School Journal 4 (March 1872):52-54; 4 (April 1872):77-78; and H. A. Thompson, "The Sunday School and the Seminary," in Third International Sunday School Convention of the United States and British American Provinces (Toronto: Executive Committee, 1890), pp. 87-100.

[34]William Reynolds, "Reports from the Field," in The Sixth International Sunday School Convention of the United States and British North American Provinces (Chicago: Executive Committee, 1890), p. 28.

[35]Quoted in Kennedy, Shaping Protestant Education, p. 41. See also Boylan, "The Nursery of the Church," p. 75; and Thompson "The Sunday School and the Seminary" who describes the church Sunday school and the church's mission Sunday school.

[36]John McCullagh, "Address by John McCullagh," in The Third National Sunday-School Convention, p. 90.

[37] Quoted in Kennedy, Shaping Protestant Education, p. 26.

[38] Kennedy, Shaping Protestant Education, pp. 30-32; Robert Lynn, Protestant Strategies in Education (New York: Association Press, 1964), pp. 15-22.

[39] Rice, Sunday School Movement, p. 89.

[40] Kennedy, Shaping Protestant Education, p. 32.

[41] Boylan, "The Nursery of the Church," pp. 86-87.

[42] Trumbull, The Sunday-School, p. 131.

[43] S. C. Bartlett, "Secularizing the Sunday School," The National Sunday School Teacher 7 (May 1872):191.

[44] See the report given by the American Sunday School Union at the Fourth National Sunday School Convention in 1869: "The American Sunday-School Union," in The Third National Sunday School Convention, p. 22.

[45] Bartlett, "Secularizing the Sunday School," p. 191.

[46] Edward Eggleston, "The Purpose" The Sunday School Teacher 3 (August 1868):227-228.

[47] Several references to this three-fold concern include J. M. Gregory, "The Aims of the Sunday School," The Sunday School Teacher 2 (May 1867):129-132; Trumbull, The Sunday School, p. 142; and Edward Eggleston, "Editor's Table," The Sunday School Teacher 2 (April 1867):125-126.

[48] See E. Morris Ferguson, Historic Chapters in Christian Education in America (New York: Fleming H. Revell Co., 1935), p. 128.

[49] S. U. R. Ford, "Sunday-School Teaching," Sunday School Journal 2 (March 1870):128.

[50] Kennedy, Shaping Protestant Education, pp. 69-71; and Malcolm Warford, The Necessary Illusion: Church Culture and Educational Change (Philadelphia: Pilgrim Press, 1976).

[51] Quoted in Kennedy, Shaping Protestant Education, pp. 58-59.

[52] Humphrey, "The National Importance of the Mission Sunday School," p. 163.

[53] Ibid., p. 162.

[54] Ibid., pp. 161, 163.

[55] J. M. Gregory, "The Future of the Sunday School," The Sunday School Teacher 2 (June 1867):173. For further expansion of this theme, see also Callene Fisk, "System in the Sabbath-school," Sunday School Journal 3 (July 1871):155-156; and Alfred Taylor, "Systematic Teaching," in The Fifth National Sunday-School Convention, pp. 124-127.

[56] Gregory, "The Future of the Sunday School," p. 178. This theme is found again and again in Sunday school literature. James A. Worden, for example, tried to demonstrate how the education of the American public could only be achieved when spiritual agenda of the Sunday school and the intellectual agenda of the common school worked together. He argued that a proper relationship only occurred when Sunday school was truly spiritual. James A. Worden, "The True Basis of Sunday-School Work," in Second International Sunday-School Convention of the United States and British American Provinces (Washington, D.C.: Executive Committee, 1878), pp. 55-61.

[57] The advancement of education method was respected as long as the method of instruction did not get in the way of the content of Christian religion. Several writers continually reminded their colleagues that an enthusiasm for method should not interfere with the spiritual ends of the Sunday school. Examples are R. G. Pardee, "Faults of Sunday Schools and Their Remedy," The National Sunday School Teacher 4 (February 1869):35-38; B. K. Pierce, "Failure of the Average Sunday-School," Sunday School Journal 2 (August 1870):243-246; and C. H. Richards, "Christian Education More than Christian Instruction," The National Sunday School Teacher 7 (July 1872):241-243.

[58] Howard Crosby, "The Philosophy of Teaching," Sunday School Journal 2 (January 1870):85; and Joseph Alden, "An Unsound Distinction," Sunday School Journal 2 (August 1870):247.

[59]H. M. Simpson, "Sunday School Teaching as a Distinct Branch of Education," Sunday School Journal 5 (January 1873):4.

[60]"The Model Sunday School Room," Sunday School Journal 2 (October 1869):11.

[61]One of the first published articles on the subject of graded classes is S. A. Taft, "Graded Bible Schools, The Sunday School Teacher 3 (March 1868):81-83.

[62]A full description of this controversy appears in E. Morris Fergusson, Historic Chapters in Christian Education in America: A Brief History of the American Sunday School Movement and the Rise of the Modern Church School (New York: Fleming H. Revell Co., 1935), pp. 146-170. More attention is given to this controversy in Chapter IV of this study.

[63]B. F. Jacobs, "The Uniform Lesson Question," in The Fifth National Sunday-School Convention, pp. 84-88. The final approval of the Uniform Lesson idea is recorded on p. 94.

[64]John Vincent, "The Supplemental Lesson," in The Second International Sunday-School Convention, pp. 79-89.

[65]John Vincent, "The Autobiography of Bishop Vincent," Northwestern Christian Advocate 58 (June 29, 1910):814. During this period, teacher education took place in what were called normal schools. The church borrowed this terminology.

[66]"Discussion on 'Teacher Training' by B. F. Jacobs," in The Third National Sunday-School Convention, pp. 126-127.

[67]Examples of various procedures for teacher training are given in the following articles: Edward Eggleston, "The True Value of Teacher Training," The Sunday-School Teacher 2 (February 1867):35-36; John M. Gregory, "Teacher's Meetings" The Sunday School Teacher 3 (July 1868):202-204; Edward Eggleston "The Teacher's General Preparation," The Sunday-School Teacher 3 (September 1868):266-268; and John Vincent in Sunday School Journal 7 (March 1875):55.

[68]"Sunday-School Normal Department," Sunday School Journal 2 (October 1869):15.

[69]A strong reminder is stated by John Vincent, "Appointing Sunday School Teachers," The Sunday School Teacher 1 (July 1866): 193-95; other examples include Edward Eggleston, "The True Value of Teacher Training," and Vincent's own expansion of this plea in "The Sunday School Teacher and the Church," The Sunday-School Teacher 2 (March 1867):73.

[70]The best introduction to the history of the development of the uniform lesson is in Lankard, American Sunday School Curriculum, pp. 201-271. See also B. F. Jacobs, "The Uniform Lesson Question."

[71]Edward Eggleston, "Editor's Table," The Sunday School Teacher 3 (December 1868):381-382 describes the progress this journal had made in only two years with its curricula "Two Years with Jesus."

[72]The Fifth National Sunday-School Convention, p. 94.

[73]By 1875, these lessons were in use by Northern Baptists, Congregationalists, Episcopalians, Lutherans, Methodists, and Moravians. Warren Randolph, "Report of the International Lesson Committee," in The First International (Sixth National Sunday School Convention) (Newark, N. J.: Executive Committee, 1875), p. 44. See also Lankard, American Sunday School Curriculum, pp. 231-233; and John Vincent, "The International Lessons," Sunday School Journal 4 (September 1872):202-203.

[74]Pardee, "Faults of Sunday Schools and Their Remedy," p. 35. See also the references under note number 57.

[75]Kennedy, Shaping Protestant Education, pp. 42-56.

[76]"The Sowing," in The Fifth National Sunday-School Convention, p. 136.

[77]"The Sowers," in The Fifth National Sunday-School Convention, p. 81. This whole section pp. 67-81 discusses the relationship of methods of teaching. Two excellent early descriptions of how the agencies of the Church are integrated with the Sunday school are L. T. Chamberlain, "The Sunday-School Work as Related to Other Agencies," in Second International Sunday-School Convention pp. 62-69; and J. A. Worden, "The Duty of the Church to the Sunday School," in Third International Sunday School Convention, pp. 114-121.

[78]Taylor, "Systematic Teaching," p. 127.

[79]Crafts, "The Pastor and the Sunday School," p. 78.

[80]Chamberlain, "The Sunday-School Work as Related to Other Agengies," pp. 62-69.

[81]Robert W. Lynn, "The Last of the Great Religious Movements," The Duke Divinity School Review 40 (Fall 1975):153.

[82]While there are many references, see for example John Hall, "Address of the Reverend John Hall, D.D." in Second International Sunday-School Convention, pp. 42-47.

CHAPTER III

THE SUNDAY SCHOOL AS THE CHURCH'S SCHOOL

The last four decades of the nineteenth century were indeed the heyday of the Sunday school. Not only was it a period of phenomenal growth, but it was a period within which an international organization was formed to propagate the idea of the Sunday school, a curriculum was developed which was widely used throughout the United States and the English-speaking world, a national system was established for Sunday school teacher education, and the first college and seminary training in religious education was initiated. The developments during this period of the Sunday school can be seen in the work of two Sunday school leaders and curriculum writers, John Vincent and Edward Eggleston. In their work for the Sunday school we see not only the form it took, but the problems and issues which had to be resolved.

John Vincent was a major architect of the Sunday school. He inspired its teacher training program and shaped its curriculum. Vincent remained a loyal supporter of the Sunday school movement until his death; for example, he delivered the major address at the 1905 convention of the International Sunday School Association projecting the future for the Sunday school in the twentieth century. Vincent was a major influence in all of the developments of the Sunday school through the last half of the nineteenth century. Edward Eggleston was also a major architect of the Sunday school and of its curriculum. Eggleston, however, was critical of many of the directions which the Sunday school took. He felt they were too extreme and were damaging its essential spiritual task. In the 1870s, Eggleston left the inner circle of Sunday school leadership and examined its progress from the outside.

Looking at the Sunday school in retrospect, Vincent could claim that significant progress had been achieved. "We remember the divine wisdom and love; we open God's Word, and, grateful for the past, look for larger and better things in the future."[1] In contrast, Eggleston warned Sunday school leaders that they had forgotten the central concerns set into the Sunday school by Robert Raikes. He argued that they were ignoring its philanthropic work, that they were teaching the mind instead of the whole pupil, and that

they mimicked the public school rather than seeking to
help pupils grow in spiritual character. He concluded,
". . . one-half of the effort put forth in Sunday-school
work is wasted, and some of it is more than wasted."2
Both sought reforms for the church's school, but
Eggleston was more cautious in his call for reform.

The Influence of Vincent and Eggleston

John Vincent's story is that of a self-education.
From being an apprentice circuit preacher, he rose to
be a Bishop in the Methodist Episcopal Church, holding
honorary Doctor of Divinity and Doctor of Laws degrees.3
He listed early home religious training, grade school,
apprentice training as an assistant circuit preacher,
a year at Newark Wesleyan Institute, wide reading and
study, and teaching as a pastor and in the Sunday
school as elements in his program of self-education.4
Such a program, he said, delivered him ". . . from the
notion that education is principally a matter of schools
and teachers, of textbooks, tasks, and recitations."5

Vincent's first adult job was as a public school
teacher, but soon after he entered the ministry, serving
as an assistant preacher on a circuit, and a city
missionary before being appointed to his first full-
time parish at Camptown, New Jersey. While as a "junior
preacher" he had had responsibility to visit and train
children and youth, his first formal involvement with
Christian education came in his parish at Irvington,
New Jersey where he instituted the "Palestine Class"
which met on Saturday afternoon to study "sacred" history, geography, and biography. The Palestine Class,
for children and adults, was sequenced into six grades--
Pilgrim to Palestine, Resident, Explorer, Dweller in
Jerusalem, Templar, and High Templar--and in it students
were examined on their learning.6 The reading of the
work of Horace Bushnell along with parish experience
convinced him that the home, church, and Sunday school
should work together to deepen faith.

He, therefore, became a lecturer on the Sunday
school, an institute teacher, and editor of The Sunday
School Teacher, one of the first periodicals to train
teachers and to advocate for a uniform lesson curriculum. By moving to Chicago, Vincent affiliated with the
"Illinois Band," a group of Sunday school leaders
headed by B. F. Jacobs and including Edward Eggleston,

who were to become architects of the uniform lesson system and of the structure of the church's school.

In 1866, Vincent was called from Chicago to New York to become an agent of the Methodist Episcopal Sunday School Union. He quickly moved up in the denomination's educational work, serving as corresponding secretary, editor of the Berean Series, and editor of publications until his election to the episcopacy in 1888.[7] From his influential educational positions, Vincent served on the executive committee of the International Sunday School Convention, was chairperson of the International Lesson Committee, and was an international spokesman for Sunday school work. By the turn of the century, Vincent's book on the Sunday school, entitled The Modern Sunday-School, was mentioned as the most significant statement of Sunday school theory and method.[8]

In addition to his general contribution to the structure of the Sunday school, Vincent was principally responsible for a system of Sunday school teacher training and the system of uniform Sunday school lessons. In the 1860s, Vincent not only started Sunday school normal work within his congregations, but also initiated the Sunday School Institute of the Northwest in Chicago. He was convinced that teacher training was the key to enhancing the educational quality of the Sunday school. As he stated,

> If the Sunday School be nothing more than a voluntary society for pious appeals to little children, especially those who lack home care and counsel, it can never become the real nursery of the church. Nor can it (under this limited theory) command the respect of adolescence nor the confidence of thoughtful and cultivated Church members. If in any sense a "school," it must be a school. It must have a strong and solid system pedagogic underneath it. The pastor must put not only his heart but his brains into it.[9]

Vincent's normal school model soon became accepted Sunday school practice. The culmination of this interest is represented in Vincent's founding of the Chautauqua Literary and Scientific Circle.[10] Begun first as a training school for Sunday school teachers, it became a vehicle for Vincent to implement his grand design of church, home, press, and school religious education.

Here Vincent embodied his concerns for education in culture and democracy.

From 1872-1896, Vincent chaired the Lesson Committee of the International Sunday School Convention. It was from this position that he advocated and shaped the curriculum which provided unity for most American Sunday schools into the first decade of the twentieth century. In The Sunday School Teacher, Vincent had demonstrated the importance of the uniform lesson notion.[11] It allowed pastor, student, teacher, and parent to unite their efforts in education. Consequently, in the Methodist Berean Series, Vincent demonstrated how a denomination could adapt the lesson system to its own use, remaining true to international unity as well as denominational integrity.[12] Since the lesson system was the primary shaper of the structure of the Sunday school through the nineteenth century, it is not surprising that Vincent was labeled one of the heroes of Sunday school work. His editor summarized the commonly held opinion of Vincent.

> In the movement for religious education of the people and especially of the young people which is now one of the movements engrossing public attention, Bishop Vincent was perhaps the greatest single influence among the pioneers. To him in very large degree is due the development of the uniform lesson system and of the International adoption of that system.[13]

He was widely known and respected for his commitment to the mission of the Sunday school as well as his efforts to improve its effectiveness.

It was Vincent who first introduced Eggleston to a significant position of Sunday school leadership. As Vincent stepped down from the editorship of The Sunday School Teacher, he introduced his successor Edward Eggleston as "the leading Sunday School man of Illinois."[14] Eggleston came to this position from Methodist pastorates in Indiana and Minnesota where he had been known as an excellent spokesperson for the Sunday school cause. In Minnesota, he had been much sought after as a lecturer and teacher of model Sunday school lessons at the state Sunday school conventions. Throughout his Sunday school work, Eggleston was committed to moving beyond the "dreariness" of the past to an improved Sunday school, but in that movement he wanted to retain

some of the old principles which he felt were crucial
for the health of the Sunday school.[15]

As an editor of The Sunday School Teacher from
1867 to 1873, he became a national Sunday school figure.
Not only did he lead that publication into national cir-
culation as the premier, non-denominational, uniform-
lesson quarterly when it became The National Sunday
School Teacher; but also he published and lectured extensively about Sunday school progress, built a model
Sunday school program at the First Methodist Episcopal
Church in Evanston, Illinois, and was responsible for
the calling of the Fourth National Sunday School Convention in 1869, the first after the Civil War. In fact
Eggleston's Sunday School Manual, published in 1869,
was recognized for several years as the definitive
text on the Sunday school.[16]

In 1873, Eggleston left the editorship of Sunday
school publications. Since 1869, he had been sharing
his time as editor of other periodicals: Little Folks,
The New York Independent, and Hearth and Home. But by
1873, Eggleston decided to devote himself exclusively
to a career in literature. His book, The Hoosier
Schoolmaster and his cultural history, History of Life
in the United States, have since become classics.
Despite this move to literature, Eggleston remained
keenly interested in the Sunday school, teaching Sunday school classes, facilitating a 1200 member church
Sunday school in Brooklyn, and periodically writing
about Sunday school progress. He was, in fact, the
person whom the editors of Scribner's Monthly asked to
write the one-hundredth anniversary address for the
founding of the Sunday school.[17]

Eggleston was convinced that the Sunday school
system needed to be improved, but he feared changes
that mirrored the public school being substituted for
the spiritual and mission core of the Sunday school.
He remained always a crusader for the original religious
aims that had sparked the Sunday school. Washington
Gladden, the famed social gospel preacher, summarized
the high esteem in which Eggleston was held.

> As a speaker at Sunday-school conventions, as a
> manager of Sunday-school teacher's institutes,
> and finally as editor of the Chicago Sunday-School
> Teacher, he made for himself a national reputation.
> No speaker was in greater request at the

anniversaries; no writer succeeded so well in impressing his ideas upon the Sunday-school workers and in getting his methods put into practice. And the best of it was that his ideas were for the most part singularly fresh, unconventional, and practicable. The cant and the claptrap of the average Sunday-school conventionist he held in infinite disgust, and stupidity and sensationalism found him an impartial foe. A very large and fruitful chapter of Edward Eggleston's life is that which describes his Sunday school work.[18]

From an analysis of the work of Vincent and Eggleston, one receives a clear picture of the structure of the Sunday school during the last half of the nineteenth century. Vincent represents the mainline Sunday school opinion; Eggleston is its friendly critic.

Addressing the Church's Sunday School

Both Vincent and Eggleston must be considered forward-looking Sunday school leaders. They were in full agreement that the Sunday school was an institution of the church. Their differences are more subtle than stark. In terms of aim, Vincent sought to promote the nursery of the church, as did Eggleston but with the reservation that the nursery of the church should include a commitment to outreach. In terms of form, Vincent sought to improve the educational quality of the Sunday school, as did Eggleston with the reservation that educational quality should never overcome spiritual vitality. In terms of scope, both sought to relate the Sunday school to the church's ministry.

The differences which emerged are most clearly revealed in each's assessment of Sunday school progress. Writing at the turn of the twentieth century, Vincent happily concluded that the Sunday school of 1900 was totally transformed. He listed ten areas of progress, most of which were concerned with form and method.[19] In terms of purpose, Vincent noted that the Sunday school had become a part of the church which served youth and adults as well as children. Its purpose and organization were fully religious. He praised denominations for actively supervising their own teaching and cooperating on an international basis with other evangelical bodies. In terms of method, he applauded the increased efforts at teacher training (particularly

Chautauqua), the architectural reform in Sunday school buildings, and the production of the International uniform lesson series which he felt had systematized the study of scripture, improved educational principles, and provided resources for teaching. In terms of scope, Vincent was pleased with the relationship the Sunday school had been building with other religious education agencies. Its concern for the enhancement of home religion was his primary example. However, he felt that the relationship with the church needed further work. The pastoral work, public worship, and societies such as Epworth League and Christian Endeavor could be better united to enhance both Sunday school and church. The changes were seen as productive and increasing the quality of the Sunday school.

In contrast, Eggleston writing on the one-hundredth anniversary of the Sunday school, presented a more ambiguous picture than did Vincent.[20] He willingly agreed that there had been progress, particularly in Sunday school method, but he feared that "the vital things" were lost in the rigid concern for method. For Eggleston, the vital things were a ". . . genuine love for childhood on the part of teachers" and a method of ". . . working by a loving sympathy in the hearts of men."[21] He was most discouraged by the intrusion of secular school models in the definition of Christian education and the development of a rigid uniform system of instruction. Both, he felt, were unrealistic and dangerous. They were unrealistic because they demanded too much of teachers. They demanded a suppression both of creativity and of the building of a human relationship for the sake of method. Both were dangerous because they set factual knowledge as the test of the Sunday school, rather than spiritual character.

> The veneering a boy with a thin respectability of hat, coat, and cane, is often the only apparent result of his attendance on Sunday-school, and it is an evil result. Let once the questions of "sacred" geography and antiquities give way to questions of practical life in Sunday-school work, and there will be less vagrancy in America. For the Sunday-school is one of the powerful formative forces in our life, and that force is sometimes perverted, and sometimes, even, tends to a genteel vagrancy.[22]

Of course, he argued, the method needed to be improved over the previous sloppy and unsystematic forms of teaching, but uniform rigidity was not the proper solution.

Such a method, he also felt, made teachers, super-intendents, and pastors forget the original mission and philanthropic purpose of the Sunday school.[23] The upbuilding of character and conversion of souls were thought to be lost in such a concern for knowledge. He called for the Sunday school to move beyond its understanding of itself as theological seminary and its "bibliolatry" to the "practical wisdom of religious living."

Eggleston, however, was also willing to admit the Sunday school's positive progress. The Sunday school periodicals and lesson systems had improved instruction and had countered those who were ". . . stranded on the sand-bars of their fogyism." The replacing of the catechism by Biblical instruction improved the focus of Sunday school instruction. Also the inclusion of volunteer teachers had not only provided a vehicle for positive service for millions of people, it had enabled them to grow in understanding other churches. Finally, the Sunday school had been able to check vices and im-prove Christian character. He, however, felt that the improvement of character would have been better en-hanced with a more thorough attention to the aim of the Sunday school rather than its method. Therefore, in Eggleston we see a forward looking judgment, but one that sought to highlight the aim of Christian edu-cation and downplay the method.

Both of these leaders were in basic agreement about aim, but they differed on the appropriate method. These differences can be seen more clearly by systematically exploring their understandings of purpose, form, and scope.

Purpose

Christian education and Christian character were the aims of the Sunday school for both Vincent and Eggleston. Vincent stated very clearly that Christian education ". . . is to be truly and intensely reli-gious, or we can dispense with it altogether."[24]

Eggleston concurred noting, "The fullest, and truest, and only correct conception of the object is that it is intended to promote CHRISTIAN EDUCATION."[25] Even the subtleties of their positions seem to be in concert with each other and mainline Sunday school theory.

Vincent, in fact, asserted that the Sunday school was "the nursery of the church" where conversion and nurture were combined. He listed conversion, religious knowledge, and Christian character as the aims of Sunday school work. In concert with his contemporaries, he emphasized Christian character as the culmination of the process.[26]

Vincent was convinced that educational process and spiritual work could unite as goals for the Sunday school. While he stated that ultimately God was responsible for salvation and the revival could be a useful tool for conversion, the process of preparation for conversion and growth in discipleship followed natural "intellectual and moral laws" which could be stimulated by education.[27]

Above all, he thought, the Sunday school was an institution of the church where children, youth, and adults were introduced to Christian experience, Christian knowledge, and Christian work.[28] It was, in fact, a primary entry point into the life of the church. Yet, for him the Sunday school took two forms. As the church's school, it was the place where Christian learning acquired in the family and from the pulpit could be focused. As the church's mission school, it provided for the poor what the family, the pulpit, and the pastorate did for the more wealthy. To quote him, "It does for the 'stranger' what the parent should do for the family."[29] The church's school worked with other agencies of religious education to inspire Christian living.

Eggleston fully agreed that Christian character was the goal of Sunday school work. Christian education was a process which included ". . . the complete development of the spiritual nature of the child."[30] Conversion therefore was the first object and character was the end. The knowledge of God's plan for life and experience in Christian living were crucial elements.

Eggleston found the theme "sowing the seed" of the Fifth National Sunday School Convention most representative of his position. The Sunday school was to sow the seed (the Word of God) until it was ready to sprout and nourish it until it was ready for harvest.[31] Eggleston claimed that the ultimate work of the Sunday school was to inspire a Christian culture. This aim was dependent on the building of Christian character-- ". . . to make the soul strong against temptation, to prepare the heart by teaching God's Word. . . . to lay the foundations of the Christian life deep and strong, to prepare the young Christian to be himself a vigorous and successful worker . . ." and this in turn was dependent on conversion.[32]

A dynamic tension was to exist between the elements of conversion, factual knowledge, and character. For Eggleston, if any of these was out of balance, Christian education was distorted. He chastized those who emphasized conversion and forgot about nurture, for they did not take seriously the total life journey of the child. He challenged those who emphasized knowledge because they failed to recognize the need for regeneration and sanctification. Character also could not be alone for it was necessarily the product of the other two.[33] In short, the Sunday school was a full evangelizing agency of the church bringing persons to God's word and helping them grow in the word.

Eggleston did advocate mission schools more forcefully than Vincent who while convinced of the importance of the mission school, actually spent most of his effort on building the church's Sunday school. Eggleston, however, thought that the distinction made between mission and church Sunday schools was false. Any Sunday school worth the name must at the same time be concerned with mission and philanthropy.

Eggleston feared that the distinction which was being made caused people to ignore the higher purpose of the Sunday school. In his caustic style, he charged that it was an attempt to keep genteel church members ". . . free from the invasion of the Goths and Vandals of the street."[34] He felt that church school theorists ignored children's need. They imposed impractical lessons, advocated Sunday school pulp at the expense of good literature, and tinkered with the Sunday school machinery instead of loving the poor. He argued that each church should have at least one mission school and that even church children would benefit more if their own schools took on a mission focus committed to the democratic principles of Christianity and the Christian

call for service of the poor. Eggleston resisted any
notion which would limit the practical benefit of the
Sunday school, and its alleviation of vice and misery.
While Vincent wholeheartedly agreed with this call, he
tended to be more secure working within the emerging
structures of the church itself.

The aim of both was to build Christian character;
yet Eggleston argued that the aim of the Sunday school
would never be fulfilled unless it was visible in practical piety and social action. Thus he sought to
determine how much vice had been checked.[35] Vincent,
on the other hand, was never as forceful in his statements. The question their differences raise is whether
the goals of church and mission education are compatible, and if so, how are they to be related?

Form

It is the issue of form which most distinguishes
these two. Eggleston was most critical of the form
which the Sunday school was taking. He believed that
this form clouded the real purpose of Sunday school
work. In their controversy is the genesis of the major
issue about the schooling-instructional model which
continues to the present.

Vincent, as most of his contemporaries, looked to
the school to provide a model for Sunday school work.
But just to say he favored a school model is not sufficient. The deeper question is how he understood the
school and what he saw as its limitations. He concluded that the day schools were progressing in their
understandings of the theory and practice of education
and were continually improving the quality of their
work with children. Not only did he feel that the Sunday school could learn from these theories, but he
feared that if the Sunday school appeared as a "poor
sister" that its power to effect Christian character
would be diminished. Therefore, he praised those who
sought to integrate learnings about the school with the
Sunday school and struggled to apply its findings.
While noting differences between Sunday and public
schools, he believed that methods of age-graded classes
with a uniform lesson, self-activity, recitation, review, and examinations were applicable to the Sunday
school.

The primary difference, he noted, between the secular and church school was the textbook used. The public school taught secular knowledge while the Sunday school taught biblical knowledge. The aim was also different with the Sunday school emphasizing moral and spiritual aims over knowledge and recognizing its dependence on divine aid. In terms of method the only differences were the power and authority of the school to enforce attendance and learning, as well as the frequency of its recitations.

Convinced of the value of the school method, Vincent however noted that this method must be subordinated to the aims of the Sunday school. The form itself was judged not to be sufficient, for he believed that even a Sunday school which was the envy of secular education-- ". . . thoroughly organized, graded, disciplined, provided with schemes of examination and or promotion . . ."--could fail if it tended toward worldliness, rather than godliness.36 The Sunday school in the final analysis was to be an agency of the church teaching church members their identity with and fidelity to the church, its worship, its mission and its "divine Head," Jesus Christ. All of the best elements of form would not suffice unless they were filled with divine grace and sought to be faithful to the divine will.

It was this conviction that led Vincent to expect the highest educational quality, the best from superintendents, pastors, and teachers. He felt God deserved the best. In the final analysis, though, it was God's grace which was crucial and which had to show through.

While he never ceased praising the contribution the school made to the church, in one of his last addresses on the future of the Sunday school he moved slightly beyond the school form. He concluded his vision of the future of the church's educational work with these words:

> The church school of the future will be less a
> school and more a home. Its keynote will not be
> recitation but conversation,--friendly conversa-
> tion. Its program will embrace, not so much
> scientific and critical studies in sacred linguis-
> tics, apologetics and systematic theology, as
> natural, simple, wisely conducted conversations
> with a view to the promotion of practical and
> spiritual life.37

Vincent saw the mutual and thoughtful conversation of friends about spiritual matters for the purpose of faithful living as the core of the Sunday school method.

Throughout his life, though, Vincent believed that the school had inspired the work of the Sunday school and that its form was not necessarily in conflict with the Sunday school aim. Eggleston, in contrast, would not agree. He felt that the aim and the form were mutually exclusive. While agreeing with Vincent's future vision, Eggleston would have argued that the vision was not possible if one took the school seriously. All the problems with Sunday school effectiveness were traced by him to a misunderstanding of the true aim of Sunday school. This misunderstanding was in turn traced to the way the word school confused Sunday school leaders. He argued that the use of the word made them seek to mirror the secular school, to impose grading, uniformity, review examinations, and the amount of information remembered as the tests for Sunday school quality.[38]

In Eggleston's view these were inadequate procedures which hid the true goal of spiritual character. In his manual on the method of Sunday school instruction, he attempted to demonstrate the need for method, the usefulness of some education ideas, and the inadequacy of a school view of the Sunday school.

> Nothing is more dangerous to the Sunday-school work than the disposition to press its methods into a constrained and unnatural correspondence with those of secular schools. The purpose and circumstances of the two are so different, that it is only in the region of general principles that this correspondence can be insisted on.[39]

The obscuring of the true aim of Sunday school work, the imposition of impractical methods, and a rigid insistance on uniformity were the results Eggleston saw from the school.

His vision of the Sunday school was close to that of Vincent's "home." He insisted on quality and seriousness, but he believed that both were only fruitful when the teacher was free to respond directly, openly,

and flexibility to the spiritual needs of the student.
Forced uniformity, which was very true of public education, was a hindrance for Eggleston. Combating uniformity is a theme which pervades his work. He pleaded
with Sunday school leaders to stop strangling the
gracious quality of the teacher and student interaction
by methods, machinery, and organization. He argued
that "healthful irregularity" is necessary for all
growth. While he did not mean to advocate no structure,
he wanted the organization to respect the freedom of
the teacher to introduce new methods and to build the
Sunday school into ". . . a living, flexible, growing
organism, not a stiff, stark, dead one."[40]

In every case, Eggleston would argue, the aim was
to determine the method, rather than the method usurp
the aim. No amount of chalk, blackboard, object lesson, or lesson help was sufficient without a genuine
love for the learner, a personal faith, and a skill
for "heartwinning."[41] The establishment of a spiritually growing relationship was the key.

The crucial differences between Vincent and
Eggleston can be seen as each attempted to apply his
theory to practice. Both insisted on improved Sunday
school facilities and better, more sincere, intellectual, and spiritual teaching.[42] They both in fact
worked in Sunday school institutes and supported plans
to build teacher training centers. But they differed
strongly on the method of uniform lessons.

Vincent seems to have been convinced by B. F.
Jacobs' uniform lesson scheme. He not only became the
chairman of the International Lesson Committee, but he
even delayed the publication of the Methodist Berean
Series so that it could coincide with the uniform
lessons. Prior to the discussion of the uniform lesson question at the Fifth National Sunday School Convention, Vincent had expressed considerable hesitation
about the idea. He had feared that it was impractical
and that it would confuse denominational beliefs in an
interdenominational system. However, by the time the
issue was voted on the floor of the convention, Vincent was thoroughly convinced. He argued that it was
practical since the Bible was its content and that it
would improve the quality of Sunday school teaching by
coordinating all of the teaching resources in a unified
way.[43] He then spent the remainder of his life working
to develop and propagate the uniform lesson curriculum.

This curriculum was judged by him to be the single most important innovation in the Sunday school; for its system united all of the educational agencies of the church around the study of the Scripture. It facilitated pastoral supervision, preaching, and worship. It increased home preparation. It strengthened teacher training and the superintendent's oversight of the Sunday school. The lesson system itself was the primary vehicle by which Christianity was protected from criticism.[44]

Vincent realized however that some flexibility was needed in the lesson system. At the 1878 meeting of the International Sunday School Convention, he presented the notion of supplemental lessons which freed some time during each Sunday lesson from the uniform lesson for denominational emphases, church history, or doctrine. It also provided time for some age-graded teaching. Nevertheless, throughout his work with the Sunday school, this material remained supplemental to the basic and central uniform Bible lesson.

He understood the need for some age grading and even advocated the teaching of the one lesson in graded classes which he called primary (five-six year olds), intermediate (seven-eight year olds), junior (ten-fifteen year olds), senior (youths), normal (for teacher preparation) and permanent (adult).[45] But never did he come to support graded instruction that used different lessons based on life needs. The unity of Bible study in appropriate classified groups with limited supplemental instruction was his vision of appropriate Sunday school method. Frankly, his notion fully coincided with the late 1900s public school notion of a uniform school system.[46]

For Eggleston, the international uniform lesson system was the primary example of the imprisonment of the Sunday school in a secular school mindset. It was a pernicious innovation. He declared, "God does not intend that all the world be whittled down to uniformity. . . . We must not expect that any two will be just alike."[47] The spontaneity of teacher and student, and the innovation of each Sunday school must be respected.

In his satirical way, Eggleston created Mr. Dogood, the superintendent of the Sunday school of the Church of Christian Endeavor of Deerfield, Illinois.[48]

69

Eggleston told how Mr. Dogood had his work cut out for
him because he had to follow the leadership of Mr.
Rutt. The real change Dogood effected though in the
Sunday school was not one of system--introducing the
"machinery" of bells, lessons, and clockwork to impose
uniformity. Rather more importantly he effected a
change in the spirit of the Sunday school. Spiritual
change, not curriculum innovation was seen as the real
need of the Sunday school.

Eggleston called the international lesson system a
"National Monopoly" where knowledge, grading, and the
quality of instruction were substituted as aims for
Sunday school work. He argued that these innovations
only succeeded to turn the bread of life, the Bible,
into a "stone." This mode of teaching, he feared,
would lead children ". . . into an aversion from truth
of Scripture itself."[49] He waited for the day it was
to be shown ineffective and was discontinued. He waited
a long time.

The criticisms of Eggleston surprised many at the
1872 convention because he had been editing a uniform
lesson periodical and had written about the value of
uniform lesson teaching. What they did not understand
was that he was not against the use of a uniform lesson in an individual Sunday school on a particular
Sunday; he was against the denominational endorsement
and imposition of a uniform lesson for all Sunday
schools across the country.[50] Each individual Sunday
school, he believed, needed some uniformity, but only
at the local level could spontaneity be protected.
Here teacher and superintendent could respond to individual spiritual needs. National uniformity usurped
the freedom of individual schools to meet particular
needs, watered down denominational distinctiveness,
made the systematic learning of Biblical facts the
order of the day, and put false content expectations on
the pulpit. A concern for uniformity and system in a
Sunday school was supported, but a national system was
challenged.

Vincent would have agreed with Eggleston when he
said that the spiritual development of children was the
aim of the Sunday school. "Let the thought be upper-
most that the Sunday-school is the children's church,
in which they are to gain spiritual nurture and
strength."[51] But, he would disagree that the uniform
lesson and the methods of the secular school turned the

70

Sunday school into a seminary or college where God's word was taught like history or arithmetic. They disagreed about the effect of the school form on the Sunday school. Their disagreement returns again and again as a basic issue for the Sunday school.

Scope

The relationship of the Sunday school to other ministries of the church and educational settings in the church were concerns for both Vincent and Eggleston. They agreed that the Sunday school was the primary, if not the only, agency where the person received a formal Christian education, and that it was not sufficient by itself to effect a full Christian life. For example, Eggleston argued the base of the Sunday school must be broadened to include the whole life of the child. What he meant, in particular, is that the Sunday school should understand the education which the child was receiving elsewhere and seek to Christianize it. "[T]hat which he gets at home, that which he gets in school, that which he gets on the street, that which he gets from books and papers . . ." were all seen as sources to coordinate and to direct in a Christian manner.[52]

Vincent was even stronger in his comments. "Here lies one of the radical defects of our modern church life. The Sunday school has turned over to it alone the responsibility of the Biblical and religious training of children."[53] Of course, Vincent saw religious training as an appropriate task for the Sunday school, but he was convinced that it was impossible without the concomitant aid of the other activities of church life. He feared that such cooperation was not often the practice in churches; therefore, he focused on the pastor as the key link and argued strongly that seminary education include training in religious education so that the pastor could more adequately perform the ministry of education. Frankly, Vincent's support of the uniform lesson series can be traced in part to his belief that it helped coordinate the Sunday school, pulpit, and family.

Vincent's vision of educational scope was indeed expansive. He hoped a system of education could be developed which unified Christian education agencies. His effort in the Chautauqua movement is an example of

71

an attempt to embody the unity. He hoped family, pulpit, pastorate, press, Sunday-school, public school, college, university, library, philanthropical organizations, clubs, and social amelioration agencies could be brought together to form a Christian education system. For both Eggleston and Vincent it was the responsibility of the church's Sunday school to coordinate this unity.

Clearly the Sunday school had been judged to be an agency of the church to educate the children of the church--to help them grow in spiritual depth and faithfulness. But the Sunday school alone could not accomplish this task. The total life of the pupil and all agencies which shaped him or her had to be included. The questions were whether the church would see this broader educational task and let the Sunday school take the lead as well as whether this Christian educational ecology could be built.

Toward the Progressive Church School

At the opening of the Second International Sunday School Convention in 1878, all of the delegates joined to sing a Sunday school march which was particularly prepared to inspire them with the importance of their work. The words of the third stanza of that march communicate the aim of the Sunday school which had become the nursery of the church. The delegates sang:

> O, give the little ones true learning
> That they may know what part to choose;
> And once the enemy discerning,
> All parley with him they'll refuse
> And O, my comrades, seek to show them
> The way to wage a deadly fight.[54]

It was this spirit of a holy cause and the desire to build a Christian culture which inspired Sunday school workers during the last half of the nineteenth century. They saw themselves waging a fight against all the forces of vice and ignorance and felt the Sunday school was a significant, if not the primary, agency in this fight.

They believed that its aim was pure, that its form was constantly progressing, and that it was instilling the culture with its democratic and Christian ideals.

72

It was with much anger and confusion that they heard
other Sunday school leaders, claiming to be progressives and Christians, say that the Sunday school was
weak and ineffective in achieving its ends. They had
committed their lives to seeing that the Sunday school
had the best form possible, that it had the best
leadership and that it worked heartily to achieve its
purpose. What they did not see and what inspired the
later progressive religious educators was how much the
methods of the public school on which they had relied
had moved beyond Sunday school practice, and how difficult it was to integrate fully the Sunday school
ministry with that of the wider church.

The Sunday school was moving into the progressive
period, but still in continuity with the past it had
set for itself. The questions of aim, form, and scope
were again being tested. Church educators asked how
well is Christian character being built, how effective
are present educational methods, and how well coordinated are the church's agencies for education? The
progressives were asking the same questions with which
the Sunday school had struggled for the last half a
century in the 1800s.

The commitments of Vincent and Eggleston are a
prelude to this transition. The issues they wrestled
with would be recounted in the next generation because
they are enduring issues for church education. Vincent
and Eggleston struggled to make the nursery of the
church an effective agency for the building of Christian
character and culture. They fully concurred with the
new definition which had been set on the Sunday school,
yet they illustrate the controversy about how this definition integrated the older mission purpose within its
aims. They fully agreed that progress had to be made
in enhancing Sunday school method, yet they illustrate
the controversy about how useful the school definitions
of educational theory and practice were. Eggleston
expressed an alternative to the characteristic practice
of his day in suggesting the school form was a detriment
to achieving Sunday school goals. Finally, they agreed
that the agencies responsible for education had to, in
some manner, be coordinated. They questioned though
how ready the church and Sunday school leaders were to
effect this cooperation. Their commitments represent
the shape the Sunday school had taken and the issues it
had to address. The progressive religious educators in

the next generation had to again respond to this definition and to these issues.

Notes

[1]John H. Vincent, "A Forward Look for the Sunday-School," in
International Sunday School Association, The Development of the
Sunday-School, 1780-1905: The Official Report of the Eleventh
International Sunday-School Convention (Boston: International
Sunday-School Association, 1905), p. 164.

[2]Edward Eggleston, "Present Phases of Sunday-School Work,"
Scribner's Monthly 19 (February 1880):531.

[3]The primary sources of information about John Vincent's life
are his autobiography which appeared as a serial in the Northwestern Christian Advocate and his statement on how he was educated which appeared in Forum. See John H. Vincent, "The Autobiography of Bishop Vincent," Northwestern Christian Advocate 58
(April 6, 1910-November 2, 1910); and Idem, "How I Was Educated,"
Forum 1 (June 1886):337-347.

[4]Vincent, "How I Was Educated," pp. 337-338.

[5]Ibid., p. 347.

[6]Vincent, "Autobiography," (June 29, 1910), p. 814.

[7]Vincent, "Autobiography," (August 17, 1910), p. 1039. See
also John H. Vincent, The Berean Beginner's Book on the International Lessons for 1888 (New York: Phillips & Hunt, 1887).

[8]See H. M. Hamill, "The Genesis of the International Sunday-
School Lesson," Henry C. McCook, "From Our Muster-Roll of Heroes,"
John Potts, "The Lesson Committee at Work," in The Development
of the Sunday-School, pp. 24-81; and W. C. Weld, "Teacher
Training," in Official Report of the Tenth International Sunday-
School Convention, ed. E. Morris Fergusson (Toledo: Executive
Committee, 1902), pp. 308-309.

[9]Vincent, "Autobiography," (August 3, 1910), p. 974. (The
first underlining is mine.)

74

[10] Vincent, "Autobiography," (July 6, 1910), p. 847.

[11] John H. Vincent, "Two Years with Jesus: A New System of Sunday School Study," The Sunday School Teacher 1 (January 1866): 13-24.

[12] John H. Vincent, "The Berean Lessons," Sunday School Journal 2 (November 1869):36-37.

[13] Charles M. Stuart, "Bishop Vincent's Autobiography," Northwestern Christian Advocate 58 (April 6, 1910):425.

[14] "Editorial Notes and Gleanings," The Sunday School Teacher 2 (January 1867):28.

[15] Eggleston's life story is told in the following books and articles: "Edward Eggleston," The National Sunday School Teacher 7 (December 1872):33-36; "Edward Eggleston: An Interview," The Outlook 60 (February 6, 1897):431-437; Washington Gladden, "Edward Eggleston," Scribner's Monthly 6 (September 1873):561-564; William Pierce Randel, Edward Eggleston (New York: King's Crown Press, 1946); and C. H. Zimmerman, "Edward Eggleston, Methodist Preacher, Novelist, Historian," The Epworth Herald 9 (March 25, 1899):706.

[16] "Edward Eggleston," p. 36.

[17] Eggleston, "Present Phases of Sunday-School Work," pp. 524-531.

[18] Gladden, "Edward Eggleston," p. 562.

[19] John H. Vincent, "The Century's Progress in Sunday-School Work," The Homiletic Review 39 (April 1900):291-297.

[20] Eggleston, "Present Phases of Sunday-School Work," pp. 524-531. See also Edward Eggleston, The Manual: A Practical Guide to the Sunday-School Work (Chicago: Adams, Blackmer, and Lyon, 1869), pp. 7-28.

[21] Eggleston, "Present Phases of Sunday-School Work," p. 529.

[22]Ibid.

[23]Ibid., p. 528.

[24]John H. Vincent, The Modern Sunday School, rev. ed. (New York: Eaton and Mains, 1900), p. 16.

[25]Eggleston, Manual, p. 5.

[26]Vincent, "Autobiography," (April 20, 1910), p. 497.

[27]John H. Vincent, The Church School and Its Officers (New York: Phillips and Hunt, 1872), pp. 23-25; and Idem, "Responsive Address," in Sixth International Sunday School Convention of the United States and British North American Provinces (Chicago: Executive Committee, 1890), p. 6.

[28]Vincent, Church School, p. 45.

[29]Ibid., pp. 43-45. See also "How Shall We Extend Our Sunday School Work?" The Sunday School Teacher 1 (July 1866): 197-198, which was probably authored by Vincent; and John Vincent, "Editor's Reply," Sunday School Journal 3 (May 1871):106.

[30]Eggleston, Manual, p. 70.

[31]Edward Eggleston, "The Epoch of Sunday Schools," The New York Independent 20 (December 10, 1868):4.

[32]Eggleston, Manual, p. 72.

[33]Eggleston, "Present Phases of Sunday-School Work," p. 530; and Eggleston, "The Epoch of Sunday Schools," p. 4.

[34]Edward Eggleston, "The Sunday School," The New York Independent 23 (March 30, 1871):2.

[35]Edward Eggleston, "The National Sunday-School Convention," The New York Independent 21 (May 6, 1869):1.

[36]Vincent, Modern Sunday School, p. 17.

[37] Vincent, "A Forward Look for the Sunday-School," p. 166.

[38] Eggleston, "Present Phases of Sunday-School Work," p. 528.

[39] Eggleston, Manual, pp. 10-11.

[40] Edward Eggleston, "Organized to Death, The Sunday School Teacher 1 (October 1866):298.

[41] Eggleston, "Present Phases of Sunday-School Work," p. 526.

[42] Their support for these improvements in the Sunday school can be found in many places. Both insisted that teachers be church members who were converted and willing to prepare themselves intellectually and spiritually for this very important task. An example of their many writing can be found in John Vincent, Sunday-School Institutes and Normal Classes (New York: Nelson and Phillips, 1872); and Edward Eggleston, "The True Value of Teacher-Training," The Sunday School Teacher 2 (February 1867):35-36. The only difference which seems to emerge is that Eggleston is more sensitive to the student's social environment, claiming that a social relationship with a student is a key to good teaching. See "Anniversary Questions," Sunday School Journal 2 (June 1870):202.

[43] "The Sowers," in The Fifth National Sunday-School Convention (New York: Aug. O Van Lennep, 1872), pp. 93-94.

[44] John H. Vincent, "Address by Bishop John H. Vincent, D.D.," in Sixth International Sunday School Convention, pp. 111-114; Idem, "Forward Look for the Sunday-School," p. 172; and Idem, Modern Sunday School, pp. 248-260.

[45] John H. Vincent, "The Supplemental Lesson," in The Second International Sunday-School Convention of the United States and British American Provinces (Washington, D.C.: Executive Committee, 1878), pp. 79-89; and Idem, Modern Sunday School, pp. 191-195.

[46] Lawrence A. Cremin, "Curriculum Making in the United States," in Curriculum Theorizing: The Reconceptualists, ed. William Pinar (Berkeley: McCutchan Publishing Corp., 1975), pp. 19-35.

[47] Eggleston, Manual, p. 107.

[48] Edward Eggleston, "Mr. Dogood's Sunday-School in Deerfield: The New Superintendent," The National Sunday School Teacher 7 (January 1872):38-39. See also Idem, "Organized to Death," pp. 297-298; Idem, "Class Teaching," in The Fifth National Sunday-School Convention, p. 121; and Idem, "Choosing a Superintendent," The Sunday School Teacher 3 (October 1868):294-296.

[49] Edward Eggleston, "Closing Exercise," in The Fifth National Sunday-School Convention, p. 147; B. F. Jacobs, "The Uniform Lesson Question," in The Fifth National Sunday-School Convention, pp. 92-93; and Eggleston, "Epoch of Sunday Schools," p. 4.

[50] Edward Eggleston, "The Fifth National Convention," The National Sunday School Teacher 7 (June 1872):236; and Idem, Manual, p. 9.

[51] Edward Eggleston, "Closing Exercises," p. 147.

[52] Edward Eggleston, "Editorial: Broader," The National Sunday School Teacher 7 (January 1872):34. See also Idem, "Address of Edward Eggleston," in The Third [Fourth] National Sunday School Convention of the United States, 1869 (Philadelphia: J. C. Garrigues, 1869), p. 118; and Eggleston, Manual, pp. 7-8.

[53] Vincent, Modern Sunday School, p. 254.

[54] "A Sunday-School March" in Second International Sunday-School Convention, p. 18.

CHAPTER IV

THE CHURCH'S SCHOOL AND THE PUBLIC SCHOOL

The Sunday school entered the twentieth century
with feelings of optimism and urgency. The optimism
reflected a sense of hope that the Sunday school could
increasingly be accepted as an essential ministry of
the church; therefore, widening its scope and influence.
The urgency reflected an underlying anxiety about
whether the Sunday school would be able to fulfill its
social task of protecting the moral and religious fiber
of the American nation. No matter how the Sunday school
grew, it never seemed to live up to its ambitions or to
match the quality of the public school. Consequently,
the story of the development of the Sunday school in
the early twentieth century is a story of sometimes
frantic, but always purposeful activity to improve the
quality of the church's educational ministry. Convinced
that the Sunday school had to create Christian character
in the American nation, had to reform its methods more
in relation to public school quality, and had to coordinate the various agencies in society which carried
elements of the religious education task, church leaders
sought to build the church school.

Criticism of the Church's Education, 1901-1922

While any periodization of history is arbitrary,
the years 1901 and 1922 represent key events in the
history of the development of Protestant education. In
1901 the first model Sunday school was established at
Teachers College in New York City. This demonstration
school attempted to model how the Sunday school could
be organized and graded in the manner of the best secular schools. It thus became a model of how excellence
could be achieved in the Sunday school and of how public
school and Sunday school were to cooperate.[1]

In 1922 interdenominational forces in Protestant
church education and denominational leadership ended
a feud which had been growing since the late nineteenth
century and combined to form the International Sunday
School Council of Religious Education which at the same
time was to respect denominational independence in educational style and content and was to coordinate denominational efforts at the practice of church education.
Leaders from both interdenominational and denominational

leadership applauded the union with the hope that it could address what was conceived as a "present emergency" in religious education and in the church. The union was asked to overcome spiritual illiteracy and check the trend toward a lower standard of morals and integrity by creating an "efficient program of Protestant Christian education."[2] Marion Lawrance, then General Secretary of the International Sunday School Association, concluded that ". . . this sort of a program will grip the churches and all the agencies that stand for moral uplift and good citizenship and unite them in the common task as they have never been united before."[3] The new council was to act as a public relations officer and educational quality inspector for the church schools.

During this period a sense of the significance of the church's educational work was renewed. Church leaders believed that the church's education redeemed and complemented public education. It gave public education a soul by providing a moral and religious purpose which was crucial for the continuation of American democracy and the American way of life. The words of President William Howard Taft to the Sixth World's Sunday School Convention in Washington, D.C. in May of 1910 reflect this belief. Taft called the Sunday school ". . . one of the two or three great instrumentalities for making the world better, for making it more moral, and for making it more religious."[4] To him Sunday school education was an essential component in the American scheme of education, complementing the secular teaching of the public school with moral and religious teaching. He concluded, "No matter what views are taken of general education, we all agree--Protestant, Catholic, and Jew alike--that Sunday-school education is absolutely necessary to secure moral uplift and religious spirit."[5]

Most educators of the church proclaimed the need for educational cooperation between public and church schools. Social progress was thought to be dependent upon a holistic form of education which included ". . . recreative, manual, intellectual, aesthetic, moral and religious" education.[6]

The church's educational contribution to the republic was therefore clarified: to build the moral and religious character of the American people so that the general welfare could be secured. While this conception

80

increased the burden on the Sunday school, it also offered a means of defending and upgrading it. As George Albert Coe commented in his Presidential address to the Religious Education Association, "The future generations in this country will be trained in religion by the churches or not at all."[7] He continued, that it was intolerable ". . . that the fragmentary opportunity that our Sunday schools now have should be largely frittered away through slipshod organizations and methods."[8] Sunday schools had an essential purpose which needed to be carried out in the most efficient and effective way possible.

At this point, Protestant church educators showed concern. They feared that this grand and essential educational purpose could fail because of faulty Sunday school method. In comparison to the public school, their institution looked too often like a joke. One popular pun of the day asked: "When is the school not a school?" The answer was, "When it is a Sunday school."[9]

Church education leaders placed the public school in a premier position. They thought that its goals were set and that the dream of universal education was becoming a reality. The common school of Horace Mann, in their minds, had achieved a truly public character. Research into child psychology had resulted in a graded curriculum developed to meet the needs of growing children. School management was developing into a science as the school organization became more bureaucratic and standardized. School buildings with separated classrooms, and instructional aids were designed. Sunday school leaders believed the progressive optimism that a better future was ahead because when ignorance was eliminated, poverty and strife would also be eliminated. Education stood as society's great hope, for it trained children for social living. The formal, irrelevant nineteenth-century school was being transformed into a school of the public.

Sunday school progressives argued that church education also needed to be transformed. Marianna C. Brown, the author of one of the first scholarly histories of the Sunday school, wrote in 1901 that the organization and methods of the Sunday school must be made comparable with the public school because Sunday school is an educational institution which deepens the meaning of the work of the public school.[10] Others

agreed with her and argued that the mismanagement of the
Sunday school weakened the nation. A. R. Taylor, the
President of James Milliken University and an important
member of the International Sunday School Association,
blamed the loss of Christian faith in many adolescents
on the failure of the Sunday school to keep in step
with the public school.[11]

It was characteristic of progressive religious
educators to identify the improvement in methods and
organization of church education as the way to fulfill
more adequately its broadened purpose. They tended to
conclude that the Sunday school organization was shoddy,
that teachers were inept, and that curriculum was inappropriate. Henry Cope, the General Secretary of the
Religious Education Association, summarized the concern
when he called the Sunday school an ". . . old-time
collection of indifferent children and ignorant teachers
meeting in the church auditorium or basement."[12]

In terms of organization, critics were appalled by
the lack of standardization among schools and the ineffective policies or superintendents.[13] That it was
not unusual for superintendents to combine classes on
Sunday because of a lack of teachers, that time was
used so inefficiently that no more than thirty minutes
were devoted to instruction, and that the class time
that remained was confused by the noise of all classes
meeting in one room were but examples of a failure of
organization.

The inadequacy of teachers was a second complaint.
Many were not competent and teacher training was, at
best, sporadic. A. F. Schauffler, of the International
Lesson Committee who had taught teacher's classes
totalling 10,000 teachers, insisted, "Teachers ought to
trust their scholars. On the average they have as good
sense as teachers and sometimes better."[14]

A third complaint was the inadequacy of buildings.
Not only did many schools meet in the basements or rooms
not suited for instruction, but most schools met in one
large assembly room where the noise of one group interfered with all others. Critics called for a building
adapted to the work of a school with separate classrooms, blackboards and a teacher's library.

Finally, critics saw the curriculum as inadequate.
Most schools were using a uniform-lesson type curriculum

where the whole student body even if divided by age studied a single lesson. Progressives charged that these curricula ignored the fact that students learn differently at different stages of psychological development.[15] They felt the curricula should be based on religious development, rather than the logical development of the lesson. A thoroughly graded scheme of lessons should be developed that adapted Biblical teachings to life and religious needs.

It seems that most of the critics agreed with J. F. Springston, a Baptist Sunday school missionary to Kansas, where he stated, "The great wonder is that our Sunday schools continue to exist in many instances."[16] Progressive church educators could not stand to see the Sunday school as an ineffective, mismanaged institution compared to the public schools; therefore, they sought to improve the form and scope of the church's education so that it could more effectively and efficiently reform its structure.

Looking to the Public School as Model

During this period church educators saw the changes which were taking place in the public school and were informed by them. As is true in the earlier periods, church educators continued to understand their school in relation to the public school. Yet, the main difference in this period is that they perceived that the public school had developed much faster than the church's school. In fact, many church leaders seemed envious of the new status which the public school was gaining, and they were depressed when they compared the Sunday school to the public school.

Their understanding of the state of public education was, however, quite idealized. In their minds the public school was moving to greater and greater pinnacles of success. They thought it had developed an excellent administrative structure, implemented graded classes and curricula, developed procedures for teacher education, and addressed the issue of the social influence of education. Public educators, and particularly the school's business critics, would not have been as optimistic. Nevertheless, the developments in public education between 1890 and 1920 were indeed significant and clearly had an influence on discussions about church education. An exploration of the

83

challenges to and response of public school education contributes to the understanding of continuity and transformation in church education.[17]

The emerging public school philosophy of education with its definition of educational structure became a model for progressive Sunday school leaders. It seemed to fit the framework which had been set for church education. This public philosophy and its form became a standard to which Sunday school purpose and form were compared and criticized. However, some of the same criticisms which were leveled at the church's educational program by progressive Sunday school leaders and some public educators were also being leveled at the public school. In the main, Sunday school leaders seemed unaware of the level of criticism which the public school faced.

The adequacy and efficiency of the public school were challenged by social progressives, public school reformers, and corporate business leaders. These critics feared that the public school was not adequately achieving its purpose of forming persons who understood and were committed to the American public mind and processes, and it was also feared that the public school was not effectively and efficiently preparing persons with the academic and industrial skills to live in urban America.

At the turn of the century, journalistic exposes were written on many American institutions. These exposes, on the whole, were written for the purpose of encouraging public officials to seek more adequately and humanely to shape social life, particularly in the city. Atrocious working conditions, political corruption, increasing crime and vice, expansionistic business practices, and exploitation of immigrants all became issues in the progressive crusade.

The school did not escape this progressive scrutiny, and in fact education and schooling received considerable examination because the school was seen as a primary institution to create a rational social order. Consistent with the American educational mythos, lack of education and of proper enculturation were seen as basic causes for social upheaval. In many ways, this argument parallels the early rationales for public schooling, that is, to create persons committed to a republican ideal and capable of contributing to life in a democracy. The state, so the rationale goes, has the responsibility to see that the citizens have the skills to be good citizens. One of the journalists who spent much time examining crime and living conditions in the urban slums, Jacob Riis, declared that the public for its own welfare and protection had ". . . to school children first of all into good Americans, and next into useful citizens."[18] In the American mind, the school had to be the leader in extending social reform and maintaining democracy.

In examining the school, critics decried inefficiency which they felt not only wasted the children's time, but also did not effectively prepare them for life in America. Liberal progressives felt that the school had not incorporated sufficiently the ideas of the child-study movement and was therefore not attending to the child as a child.[19] Until the interests of the child were addressed, they felt the school could not provide adequate modeling of the community at large, and train the child in the responsibility of a person in that community.

The adequacy of teachers was itself an issue. The last three decades of the nineteenth century had seen much activity to improve the quality of normal education for teachers, but it did not seem enough. Joseph Rice in his The Public-School System of the United States highlighted the inadequacy of teachers when he wrote, "The office of teacher in the average American school is perhaps the only one in the world that can be retained indefinitely in spite of the grossest negligence and incompetency."[20] The school was challenged to improve significantly the quality of its instruction. To do so demanded increased teacher competence.

School organization was also severely challenged during the first five decades of the twentieth century. Efficiency had become the watchword for business, and its discipline, "scientific management," was introduced in school criticism. The cost of the school when compared to its actual effect was described, in some circles, as a story of robbery and plunder.[21] School administrators were challenged to demonstrate what goals motivated the schools, how they were being met, how the system efficiently functioned, and more importantly how children were being prepared for full participation in American society. The push for vocational education is but one example of the attempt to relate the public school more intimately to social life and work.

85

These challenges to the public school by progressives were really in the mood of a lover's quarrel. The progressives were convinced that the public school was crucial to the realization of American public reform. They wanted to improve this essential institution. As Lawrence Cremin has argued in his history of progressive education,

> . . . progressive education began as part of a vast humanitarian effort to apply the promise of American life--the ideal of government by, of, and for the people--to the puzzling new urban-industrial civilization that came into being during the latter half of the nineteenth century. The word <u>progressive</u> provides the clue to what it really was: the educational phase of American Progressivism writ large.[22]

Through this movement, Cremin argued, the school was transformed into an institution central to maintaining, transmitting, and transforming the American way of life. It was guided by professional school administrators and professional teachers, and committed to assisting the individual child in creating a place for himself or herself within the American community. Cremin details the commitments held in common by progressive educators: (a) a broadening of the purpose of public schooling into family and community life, (b) the relating of research in the human sciences to classroom pedagogy, (c) the development of procedures of instruction tailored to different class and vocational interests, and (d) the attempt to mediate high culture in a democratized form to children.[23]

The public school was therefore not the pure institution which many Sunday school leaders thought it was. Public school leaders had to respond to the criticisms of their work. It was these responses which Sunday school leaders followed closely in their attempts to use public education to transform church education. At the turn of the century, public school educators began to extend the curriculum of the school, to upgrade the quality of teachers, and to make the system of public school instruction more efficient. In fact, the school did move in this period to a more central role in American society. The expansion of the laws enforcing compulsory school attendance is an example. In 1890 only twenty-seven states and territories had required school attendance, but by 1918 every state had required schooling until at least twelve years of age and several even until sixteen years of age. It was also increasingly being felt that children needed more than an elementary education; therefore, high schools were expanded.

Graded classrooms and curricula are one significant example of how the public school sought to respond to calls for an increased agenda. Graded classrooms were introduced for two sometimes contradictory reasons in the period from 1870 to 1910: (a) to improve the system of the public school, and (b) to address the needs and interests of individual children. The first major graded system of instruction can be traced to William Torrey Harris' St. Louis school system.[24] Harris saw grading as a rational way of sequencing instruction and judging whether pupils were satisfactorily progressing through the schools. Graded classes enabled Harris to structure curriculum into units of instruction which could be taught by teachers and tested in the school board exams. Grading therefore provided the system so that children learned what they needed to learn in the appropriate sequence to make appropriate progress in the system. Instruction was sequenced more in terms of the system's needs, rather than the children's needs.

Also for other reasons, the idea of classifying pupils came to make much sense to liberal educational leaders. It provided a method to respond to the fact that children have different capabilities to learn that progress with age. The work of Francis Wayland Parker, first in the Quincy, Massachusetts school system and later in Chicago, to put the individual interests and needs of the child in the forefront combined with the psychological research of the child-study movement were particularly instrumental in developing a system of public school instruction and curriculum which sequenced instruction in terms of the growing needs of the child.[25] The hope was to model the child's natural process and potential for learning in the school. The school was to function as a microcosm of the world and to prepare children for the world. In Parker's words, the school was structured as ". . . a model home, a complete community and embryonic democracy."[26] While the needs of the child were highlighted, they were seen in relation to the needs of society.

87

The full embodiment of a graded school based on child-study came in 1896 when John and Alice Chipman Dewey established "The Laboratory School" in Chicago.[27] Soon to become a part of the University of Chicago, this school was a total educational environment with classes from kindergarten through high school, sequenced to provide a continuous developing path from the home and neighborhood through to college and work. Each age level was given different tasks based on child-study research. For example, in terms of science the curriculum moved from study of plants and animals, to geography, to the tools of society (electricity, telephone, telegraph). The child was also to experience school as parallel to real work. Through hard work such as carpentry, sewing, cooking, etc., the child was to come to experience life, and, through school social organization and decision making, the child was to experience democracy.[28] At the core, the school was to guide pupils to full participation in American democracy. As Cremin states, "Dewey saw the main line of a curriculum that was scientific in its view of the child and progressive in its effect on society."[29]

In addition to the sequencing of instruction, the scope of the curriculum expanded. Kindergartens were formed to provide a means of enriching the child's early training, high schools became mass training institutions by 1920 with various tracks for different vocational interests, and vocational schools were created to lead children directly into productive work. Dewey, for example, argued that the school should become a full microcosm of society.[30] Thus curricula were created which attempted to combine the educational needs of the child and the needs of society into an ordered pattern of instruction. While on the one hand some Dewey followers would break this relationship and emphasize the child as primary, the public schools themselves tended to emphasize the needs of society. Education was deemed effective when it was based on child needs, and when it formed children for productive roles.

The professionalization of education is a second example of the response of the public school. The effort was to improve teacher expertise and adequately integrate the teacher's function into the society's educational task. The National Education Association (NEA) had been founded in the late 1860s as support for the sharing of educational information and particularly as a support for the education of teachers. From then on normal schools increasingly emerged as the means of preparing teachers. Yet, the full acceptance of the idea was not realized until the last of the nineteenth century with real progress signaled by the formation in 1887 of Teachers College in New York as a model teacher training facility. A professional definition of teaching rapidly developed in the 1890s. As Cremin describes it, the progressives saw the teacher as ". . . an artist of consummate skill, properly knowledgeable in the field, meticulously trained in the science of pedagogy, and throughly imbued with a burning zeal for social improvement."[31] The progressives encouraged professionalization in teaching. As was true in other areas of life, the highest quality training was thought needed to fulfill effectively calls for social progress. Schools of medicine, law, pedagogy, and even ministry became the means to train the professionals, the doctor, lawyer, teacher, and minister. Each was given an identity as a professional. Such a movement defined a relationship between those with skills and the consumers of their products with the belief that service would be more effectively delivered.

Within the professions themselves a hierarchy of subspecialities was formed. In education this meant the university professor of education conducted research into the public function and responsibility of education, the school administrator (who came into "his" own in the 1910s) applied and organized education to fulfill the public responsibility, and the teacher instructed children in the skills of social living. Even within teaching itself a hierarchy developed of college teacher, high school teacher, and children's teacher. Professionalism sought to define expertise, improve quality, inspire social progress, and judge effective practice. The teacher and school official who emerged during the early twentieth century looked much different from their predecessors. The professional school for educators sought to combine research and public service to enhance the quality and responsiveness of school organization, curriculum production, and classroom instruction.

A third example of the response of public education can be seen in the movement to improve school organization. Harris' model of bureaucratic centralization had become a primary form for public education in urban areas by the 1880s. While it could not be extended to rural areas on a large scale before the 1920s, it was nevertheless still considered the primary framework for school administration. The actual ingredients of Harris' model were significantly changed between 1880 and 1920; yet the basic conceptualization remained intact. Bureaucratic centralization became the "one best system," to quote David Tyack.[32] Tyack describes how school leaders were influenced by transformations in industrial America. The factory of the nineteenth century provided the primary model for effecting centralization until replaced in the early twentieth century by the corporation. Both emphasized unity, rationality, and social control.

The school of the late nineteenth century, Harris' school, for example, sought to mirror the effective form of the factory. The elements of the factory-- division of labor, order, punctuality, and regularity-- became the elements for the school system. The urban school was headed by a superintendent who, while accountable to an elected lay school board, structured the system into districts, divided pupils into classes, sequenced a curriculum in textbooks to be administered uniformly by teachers, and tested the quality of teaching and learning through examinations.[33] The goal was to create a "well-oiled" and controlled system of production which yielded "young scholars."

The bureaucratic school was an attempt to improve previous modes of school organization which were often idiosyncratic and politically motivated. The goal of those who insisted on the bureaucratic model was to protect schools from capricious political decisions, instill order and system, and place those with expert knowledge in charge. The movement to professionalize the system therefore emerged as a reform movement in the 1870s as a response to increased demand on schools in growing urban areas. But by 1900 the "factory form" no longer seemed effective to meet those goals of professionalization and reform. It seemed too rigid and uniform. Tyack has shown that administrative progressives saw a need for a more responsive and comprehensive approach. "They were evangelists for new education goals of science and social efficiency. They still wanted a one best system, but it was to be a more complex, differentiated organization adapted to new social and economic conditions."[34]

The "modern" business corporation seemed a much more adequate form. It centralized control even further into the hands of professionals and attempted to improve the efficiency and flexibility of urban education. Schools were to be organized according to the sciences of education and management with professionals with expertise defining procedures. Specialists were created to fulfill particular responsibilities in an increased division of labor; for example, there came into being vocational education specialists and curriculum specialists. Educational tracks, special programs, and new subjects for instruction expanded curricula. Education was asked to respond to individual needs and develop a socially-productive student.

Education was put to the business tests: was it efficiently run, did it eliminate waste, did it produce learning at the cheapest cost? Educational administrators became modeled after business leaders. In his history of the development of the profession of education administration, Raymond Callahan tells how the decade from 1910 to 1920 was crucial as educational leaders defined themselves in terms of business convictions and strategies.[35] The tests for adequate education became efficiency, productivity, and profit. The educational administrator became more a manager and less an educator in this division of labor. Efficiency tests and standards for the school system and teaching were set, and procedures were established to account for the cost of public education.

In terms of procedures, great changes resulted in the educational system. The old "one best system" had indeed been transformed, but it was still a "one best system." The conception of bureaucratic centralization not only remained, but was enhanced in the move to the corporate business model.

In terms of curriculum, teacher professionalization, and school organization, the public school changed significantly from the 1880s to the 1920s. Yet underlying these changes was a basic continuity. The purpose of the school remained to form persons into effective participants in the American social order. The form chosen to effect this purpose was a revision and intensification of the model of bureaucratic centralization. School leaders felt that many of the criticisms were accurate, and they desired to respond appropriately. Yet in their response and with an urgent mood of change, they really acted out of a past conceptualization. Both change and continuity are evident in their response.

91

The Public School and the Church's School

The new curricula, the new modes of school management, the new strategies for teacher education, and the new responsiveness of public education seen in the area of specialization were intriguing to church leaders. Church educators saw the need for change and attempted to effect it. The seriousness with which they took the transformation in public education is reflected in the major innovations that occurred in church education during the first two decades of the twentieth century. Of course, the creation of a demonstration Sunday school at Teacher's College is one example. It was a clear attempt to effect a cooperation between public and church education and to build a school for the church parallel to the public school. Five other major innovations reflect how the church educators borrowed from their public school counterparts in transforming the Sunday school into a true school of the church: (a) the founding of the Religious Education Association in 1903 to provide a forum for integrating educational research into the church's program, (b) the formal acceptance by the International Sunday School Association of the idea of a thoroughly age-graded curriculum in 1908, (c) the formation of the Sunday School Council of Evangelical Denominations in 1910 to coordinate denominational efforts at educational reform, (d) the first official use in 1911 of the phrase, "School of the Church," as a substitute for the name "Sunday school," and (e) the initial adoption of educational standards of excellence for church schools in 1911. Each of these five changes reflect the emerging consensus about the practice of Protestant Christian education.

The clearest example of the effort at transformation is seen in the activity of researchers in education and religious education to form a professional organization to explore in depth and with academic rigor issues of religious education. In 1903, after much struggle, the Religious Education Association (REA) was founded. This organization grew from tentative beginnings to become a major force in research in religious education. Imbued with a commitment to a public pedagogy which sought to unite the forces of education for the benefit of the nation, its stated purpose, accepted in 1905, was

. . . to inspire the educational forces of our country with the religious ideal: inspire the

religious forces of our country with the educational ideal: and to keep before the public mind
the ideal of Religious Education and the sense of
its need and value.[36]

Throughout the first decades of the journals of REA,
one sees a continuing commitment to a partnership between secular and religious education for the benefit
of the public.[37] One also sees both the hope and the
frustration--a hope that the potential of the Sunday/
church school could be realized and a frustration at
the effort it took to shape it into a real school.
REA functioned to maintain the holistic vision and to
inform the church of the best research in education.

Individual denominations responded to the challenge to form a truly effective church education program first by lobbying for a thoroughly graded curric-
lum series which would present the Biblical story in
relation to educational and psychological research,
and then by forming in 1910 the Sunday School Council
of Evangelical Denominations, as a means of coopera-
tively improving the actual practice of denominational
education.[38] They hoped to stand for a higher standard
of education which broke from patterns of the past.
The council was to be avowedly educational in its
agenda.

The inevitable acceptance of the notions of educational improvement in the churches is therefore reflected in the merger of the council and the International Association in 1922. Without commitment to
educational change, this would not have been possible.
In the twelve years from 1910-1922, both organizations
had come to agree that the vehicle for the church's
education was the church school and that high standards
of educational excellence were needed for both church
practice and curriculum construction. By the end of
the second decade of the twentieth century, the education committees of both groups were not only chaired
by the same person, Walter Athearn, Professor at Boston
University, but both had agreed to common standards for
age-level work and teacher training, to the notion of
community coordination of agencies of religious education, and to age-graded, life-centered curricula.[39]

The church school became a full-fledged conception
in the second decade of the twentieth century. What
the Northern Baptists had begun officially in 1911 to
call the "School of the Church" became a reality for

mainline Protestantism.[40] No longer was the Sunday
school an instructional activity limited to Sundays
with limited educational quality. It was becoming the
effort of the Church to coordinate a variety of instructional activities and to teach in a competent manner
religious faith, religious action and the moral resources for American democracy.

These five innovations demonstrate how the public
school had become an ideal for many church education
leaders. The understanding of the success of the public
school which these leaders had stimulated them to
criticize their own school and to struggle to revise
the Sunday school into a true school of the church--with
a religious purpose, but with an effective educational
method. Hugh S. Magill, a field secretary of the REA
and soon to become general secretary of the International Council of Religious Education, summarized the
relationship in his 1922 address to the last convention
of the International Sunday School Association. Entitled "A Comprehensive Program of Education, Secular
and Religious," Magill argued that there had been an
intimate relationship of public and religious education
throughout American history. Here the religious purpose of all education had combined with the public need
to develop good citizens in building a comprehensive
program of education. Such a goal demanded, he felt,
that both public and religious education be as effective,
professional and competent as possible.[41] A graded
curriculum, well-trained teachers, adequate funding and
an efficient system were listed as the essential elements of a church school that could be conducted in a
cooperative relationship with the public school--a goal
which he held as crucial.

The public school and the church school were seen
as partners; therefore, one cannot discuss developments
in Protestant church education in the early twentieth
century without concurrently discussing developments
in the public school. In analyzing their institution,
church educators sought to learn from what they perceived as positive changes in the public school. Such
a borrowing suggests that the church's experience
would be similar to that of the public school--change
would be experienced in the midst of a prevailing
structure. A closer examination of the experience of
church education does in fact demonstrate that the
experience was similar.[42] Just as public educators
sought to transform their institution, so did church
educators; but just as public education change must be

94

seen in light of the continuity of purpose and form, so must church education. The public school and the church school continued the trend of developing in a sympathetic relationship in structure as well as in content.

Notes

[1]Richard Morse Hodge, "The Model Sunday School at Teachers College," Religious Education 1 (April 1906):140-142.

[2]Report of Committee on Education of the International Sunday School Council of Religious Education (Kansas City: International Sunday School Council of Religious Education, 1922), pp. 5-8. See also "Plan of Reorganization," in International Sunday School Association Organized Sunday School Work in North America, 1918-1922: Official Report of the Sixteenth International Sunday School Convention, ed. Herbert H. Smith (Chicago: International Sunday School Council of Religious Education, 1922), pp. 73-86; and Sunday School Council of Evangelical Denominations, Minutes, Twelfth Annual Meeting (Toronto: George Webb, Secretary, 1922), p. 7.

[3]Marion Lawrance, "Secretary's Report," in Organized Sunday School Work, 1918-1922, p. 110.

[4]William Howard Taft, "The President's Estimate of the Sunday-School," in World's Sunday School Association, World-Wide Sunday School Work: The Official Report of the World's Sixth Sunday-School Convention, ed. William H. Hartshorne (Chicago: The Executive Committee of the World's Sunday-School Association, 1910), p. 125.

[5]Ibid.

[6]"The Rochester Convention," Religious Education 2 (April 1907):25. This theme of holistic education and its significance for social progress is repeated many times through the first three decades of the twentieth century. Other examples of references are Nathaniel Butler, "The Moral and Religious Element in Education," Religious Education 1 (June 1906):93; George Albert Coe, "Annual Survey of Progress in Religious and Moral Education," Religious Education 4 (April 1909):15; and Ernest Bourner Allen, "The Sunday School and the Nation," in World's Sunday School Association, World-Wide Sunday-School Work, p. 145.

[7]George Albert Coe, "The President's Annual Address: New Reasons for Old Duties," Religious Education 5 (April 1910):4.

[8]Ibid., p. 5. See also B. S. Winchester, "The Next Thing in Religious Education," in International Sunday School Association, Organized Sunday School Work in America, 1908-1911: Official Report of the Thirteenth International Sunday School Convention (Chicago: International Sunday School Association, 1911), p. 327.

[9]Reported in Robert Lynn and Elliott Wright, The Big Little School: Sunday Child of American Protestantism (New York: Harper & Row, 1971), p. 75.

[10]Marianna C. Brown, Sunday-School Movements in America (New York: Fleming H. Revell Co., 1901), pp. 190-191.

[11]A. R. Taylor, "The Relation of the Sunday-School to the Public School," in International Sunday School Association, The Development of the Sunday School, 1780-1905: The Official Report of the Eleventh International Sunday-School Convention (Boston: International Sunday School Association, 1905), p. 189.

[12]Henry Frederick Cope, The Modern Sunday School in Its Present Day Task (New York: Fleming H. Revell Co., 1907-1916), p. 12.

[13]See Martin C. Brumbaugh, "The Need of Trained Teachers," in World's Sunday School Association, World Wide Sunday-School Work, p. 468; and E. A. Jones, "The Public School and the Sunday-School," in International Sunday School Association, Organized Sunday School Work in America, 1905-1908: The Official Report of the Twelfth International Sunday School Convention (Chicago: International Sunday-School Association, 1908), p. 624.

[14]A. F. Schauffler, "The Better Organization of the School," in The Hundredth Year: The Story of the Centenary Celebration of the Sunday School Union, 1903, ed. M. Jennie Street (London: The Sunday School Union, 1903), p. 60.

[15]This theme was treated by many church school leaders, for example see W. Douglas MacKenzie, "Graded Lessons," in International Sunday School Association, Organized Sunday School Work, 1905-1908, p. 529; Jones, "The Public School and the Sunday-School," p. 624; and Samuel B. Haslett, The Pedagogical Bible School: A Scientific Study of the Sunday School with Chief Reference to the Curriculum, 3rd ed. (New York: Fleming H. Revell Co., 1903), pp. 1-2.

[16]J. D. Springston, "The Application of Modern Educational Theory to the Work of the Sunday School," Religious Education 3 (August 1908):90.

[17]The following interpretation of the history of late nineteenth and earlier twentieth century public education is indebted to the revisionist public school historians, particularly Michael Katz, Class, Bureaucracy and the Schools: The Illusion of Educational Change in America, expanded ed. (New York: Praeger Pub., 1975); and David B. Tyack, The One Best System: A History of American Urban Education (Cambridge: Harvard University Press, 1974). For a critique of the revisionist school, see Diane Ravitch, The Revisionists Revised: A Critique of the Radical Attack on the Schools (New York: Basic Books, 1978).

[18]Jacob A. Riis, The Children of the Poor (New York: Charles Scribner's Sons, 1892), p. 8. See also his The Battle with the Slum (New York: Macmillan Co., 1902).

[19]Of course the best examples of this criticism can be seen in the work of Francis Wayland Parker and John Dewey. See for example Francis W. Parker, Talks on Pedagogies: An Outline of the Theory of Concentration (New York: A. S. Barnes & Co., 1894); John Dewey, The School and Society, 3rd ed. (Chicago: University of Chicago Press, 1900); and Idem, The Child and the Curriculum (Chicago: University of Chicago Press, 1902). Perhaps the best feel for educational response to the criticisms can be seen in John and Evelyn Dewey's Schools of Tomorrow (New York: E. P. Dutton Co., 1915). Here the Deweys illustrate creative educational responses in the first years of the twentieth century. The principle of education for democracy is primary. For them the new spirit in education prepared ". . . children for the life they are to lead in the world" and it embodied ". . . the needs and conditions of a democratic society" (p. 288). See Chapter XI on Democracy and Education.

[20] Joseph Mayer Rice, The Public-School System of the United States (New York: Century Co., 1893), p. 15.

[21] For a description of this critique of schooling see Raymond E. Callahan, Education and the Cult of Efficiency: A Study of the Social Forces that have Shaped the Administration of the Public Schools (Chicago: University of Chicago Press, 1962).

[22] Lawrence Cremin, The Transformation of the School: Progressivism in American Education 1876-1957 (New York: Alfred A. Knopf, 1961; New York: Vintage Books, 1964), p. viii.

[23] Ibid., pp. viii-ix.

[24] See the interpretation of Robert Church about the reasons for grading. Education in the United States: An Interpretive History (New York: Free Press, 1976), p. 85, 251-260.

[25] See Cremin, Transformation of the School, pp. 127-135.

[26] Parker, Talks on Pedagogies, p. 450.

[27] For a description of the school see Katherine Camp Mayhew and Anna Camp Edwards, The Dewey School: The Laboratory School of the University of Chicago, 1896-1903 (New York: D. Appleton-Century Co., 1936).

[28] See Dewey, School and Society, pp. 113-129. The last chapter is devoted to a description of the first three years of the laboratory schools and its innovations.

[29] Cremin, Transformation of the School, p. 141.

[30] John Dewey, Democracy and Education (New York: Macmillan Co., 1916), p. 92.

[31] See Cremin's description of the founding of teacher's college in Transformation of the School, pp. 170-176. See also Burton Bledstein, The Culture of Professionalism: The Middle Class and the Development of Higher Education in America (New York: W. W. Norton & Co., 1976).

[32]Tyack, The One Best System, pp. 5-12. Much of the following description is drawn from Tyack's excellent research.

[33]Ibid., pp. 42, 50.

[34]Ibid., p. 188.

[35]Callahan, Education and the Cult of Efficiency, particularly chapters 5 and 8.

[36]"The Purpose of the Association," Religious Education 1 (April 1906):2.

[37]See for example William Fraser McDowell, "The President's Annual Address," Religious Education 1 (April 1906):9. See also Stephen Schmidt, "A History of the Religious Education Association," Chicago, 1982 (photo-copied).

[38]MacKenzie, "Graded Lessons," pp. 524-531. See also E. Y. Mullins, "What the International Sunday-School Association Stands For," in Organized Sunday-School Work, 1905-1908, pp. 16-17; Sunday School Council of Evangelical Denominations, Minutes, Third Annual Meeting (New York: Office of the Secretary, 1913), p. 1; and in the same volume "Constitution: The Sunday School Council of Evangelical Denominations," pp. 70-73.

[39]See Henry H. Meyer, "Report of the Secretary," in Minutes, Third Annual Meeting, pp. 24-25; and "Educational and Extension Section," in Sunday School Council of Evangelical Denomination, Minutes, Sixth Annual Meeting (Philadelphia: George T. Webb, Secretary, 1916), pp. 29-63.

[40]Henry Frederick Cope, "Ten Years Progress in Religious Education," Religious Education 8 (June 1913):126.

[41]Hugh S. Magill, "A Comprehensive Program of Education, Secular and Religious," in International Sunday School Association, Organized Sunday School Work in North America, 1918-1922, p. 162.

[42]The actual ways in which church education borrowed from public education will be discussed in the section on form in Chapter V.

CHAPTER V

BUILDING THE CHURCH SCHOOL

In 1922 when the Sunday School Council of Evangelical Denominations united with the International
Sunday School Association, leaders in the church education world felt that a new day had been born. During
the previous two decades the conception of the church
school had been invented and procedures defined to
build it. The struggle for the church school had renewed progressive church educators; yet, they were
still anxious because the transformation of the Sunday
school into the church school had not been as rapid
and effective as they had hoped.

The agenda which was set for the International
Sunday School Council of Religious Education in 1922 is
a summary of the issues defined for church education in
the early twentieth century and a description of the
vision church educators hoped to create. The council's
Committee on Education summarized the concerns which
needed response: (a) millions of children were un-
reached by the church, (b) inadequate time was given to
church education, (c) church school teachers and
officers were untrained and unsupervised, (d) the curriculum was inadequate, (e) the housing and support of
the Sunday school were meager, (f) home religious education was declining, and (g) a rivalry existed among
the agencies attempting to carry the church's education.[1] As is obvious, many of these issues paralleled
concerns which emerged much earlier in Protestant church
education, and many were influenced by public education.

The committee members were convinced that the
church had the obligation to be an effective partner in
the education of the public. They endorsed a 1921
resolution of the National Council of Education as
their platform.

> In view of the dependence of democracy upon
> religion, and the attacks to which all churches
> and all democratic governments are alike being
> subjected by radicals and emissaries of nations
> now under radical control: it is the duty of all
> churches, irrespective of differences of creed,
> to unite in an effort to make religious education
> more universal and efficient, to emphasize demo-
> cratic elements in religious instruction, and to
> correlate religious instruction with all elements

101

in public school education helpful to religion;
. . . and it is the duty of churches and public
schools alike to make earnest effort to ensure a
more general reverence for divinity and respect
for all things religious, including respect for
churches other than one's own and for everything
connected with their forms of worship.[2]

The belief that the spiritual ideals of the church and
democratic virtues of citizens must be promoted together inspired their rhetoric and action. Hugh Magill,
the new general secretary of the International Council,
stated the conviction starkly. In addition to "bringing
the gospel of truth to every soul," the task of the
church is now ". . . supplemented by the patriotic
motive of instilling in the hearts and minds of the
American youth those religious principles which give
sanction and support to the moral elements necessary to
good citizenship, and the preservation of free government."[3]

     To fulfill such an agenda the new International
Council agreed with Walter Athearn's notion to two
parallel school systems, one the public school and the
other a church religious school. Both were to be based
on the highest principles of the science of education,
organized according to the best methods of educational
administration, staffed with the most competent and
professional teachers and leaders, and committed to
sympathetic cooperation.[4]

     Nevertheless these church leaders highlighted that
religious education had an unique technique and content
built on religious experience. Consequently, they encouraged further research into the unique character of
religious education. Challenging particularly the
behaviorist and pragmatic philosophies which dominated
the public schools, they instructed the council to support the development of a profession of religious education, encourage coordination of agencies for religious
instruction, and improve teachers and leaders.

     It is important to look at how the consensus and
feelings of hope and new possibility formed in these
two and one-half decades. The purpose, form, and
scope of Protestant education must again be examined.
The feeling and fact of the new must be seen in relation
to the persistence of the older Protestant education
framework.

The Purpose of the Church School

In the middle of the nineteenth century the Sunday school had moved from an institution external to the church to an institution of the church with the expressed purpose of introducing persons to the Christian faith and helping them to grow in faith and understanding. The ultimate goal of the Sunday school process was to instill Christian character in persons, and thereby influence American culture toward Christianity. The nursery of the church was to be the nursery of Christian character.

This nineteenth century agenda was intensified throughout the first decades of the twentieth century-- to such an extent in fact that in the later 1930s and 1940s some neo-orthodox critics were to challenge that the Sunday school had lost its soul to American culture. They argued that the concern for morality and American democracy had co-opted the iconoclastic nature of prophetic Christian faith.[5] Even these critics, however, would not have denied Christian character as an agenda, and their criticism stands as evidence for the inextricable relationship of church and culture in definitions of education. Their version was just more critical of the cultural context of American Christianity.

Progressive Christian educators felt they were in partnership with public educators to protect American culture and to give it a Christian soul. The description of this cooperation continued the earlier Protestant expansionism. Dialogue with other religious traditions, particularly Jewish, was engaged, but the Protestant definition of social life remained predominant. This conviction can be seen throughout the literature of religious education in this period. The proceedings of the International Sunday School Association, the journal of the Religious Education Association, and the minutes of the Sunday School Council of Evangelical Denominations alike record this agenda. For example, one of the early Presidents of the Sunday School Council, William Funk, declared in 1913 that we need to work ". . . so that the strong arm of the Church may be about and beneath the Sunday-school life of the denominations to hold it steady until Christian character has been fully established, being rooted and grounded in Him."[6] His words were echoed by B. S. Winchester in an address to the Thirteenth Convention

of the International Association who declared that
America is engaged in an experiment in mass education
for democracy and citizenship with the church.[7] Also,
the Religious Education Association (REA) reflected
this agenda in the 1913 report of its committee on the
correlation of educational agencies of the local church
where the goals of the church school were described as
helping people love and worship God, realize the
Christian ideal in their character, and embody that
ideal in their public life.[8] Not only were an individual's actions to be changed, but also those of the
society at large. Education was the foundation from
which the church attempted to extend God's kingdom.

Progressive educators argued that no institution
of society could or ought to take the responsibility
of the church for religious education. It was therefore no accident that they began to call the Sunday
school the school of the church or the church school.
By doing this, they did not deny that other institutions in society also carried the tasks of religious
and moral education, for example, the YMCA and YWCA;
nevertheless, they affirmed that the church was to be
responsible for the co-ordination and evaluation of that
total process of Christian education.

In the literature four reasons can be found which
were used to demonstrate that the church was the only
agency able to fulfill this agenda. In the first
place, it was agreed that the church was the ". . .
agency for fostering and expressing the religious
life."[9] Secondly, the school was unable to teach
religion effectively because of the doctrine of the
separation of church and state. Third, the complexity
of American society demanded a process of education
more significant and complex than the home or previous
informal processes of religious education could provide.
Last, the church was the only American institution with
enough of a holistic vision to see the various ways
religion was taught in society, and thereby able to
provide a unifying and co-ordinating center to this
complexity.[10] Consistent with the earlier vision of
Protestant education, the vehicles of religious education were made responsible to the church; and in turn,
the church was responsible to see that the program was
adequately conceived, funded, monitored, and evaluated.

It is true that in this period the language of
salvation was used less frequently to describe the purpose of the church school; yet the words Christian

104

character and Christian culture were to carry the same meaning. It was assumed that salvation was a prerequisite for church membership; therefore, to speak of creating citizens who were both American and Christian meant creating citizens who were saved and who struggled to live a saved existence. Most progressive educators did not talk about the act of salvation, rather they spoke of creating a church context where salvation was nurtured. Most of the new curriculum material included a time, usually in middle adolescence, when youth were to claim the salvation which had been nurtured by the church.[11] Furthermore, most progressive educators were careful to highlight the religious character of their work.

Of course, the word salvation is highly nuanced, as are the words Christian character and culture, and they can be used in a variety of ways. Nevertheless, both twentieth-century church educators as well as nineteenth-century Sunday school leaders agreed that their task was to effect salvation--to help persons become Christian in order that their actions would be consistent with Christian faith. They differed on the processes with some seeing salvation as a specific moment and others seeing it as a nurturing process, but effecting Christian living in American life was a common agreement. Christian education was described as a religious activity, controlled by the church to build the church, to train its leaders, and to prepare its members to influence public life. The nursery of the church was reaffirmed.

The Form of the Church School

Again, as was true in the earlier period, the church looked to innovations in public education as potentially providing solutions to problems of form and method. In church education the same transition as that which took place in public education is evident. Between 1900 and 1920 the conception of the church school changed from a factory to a corporate model, but a basic bureaucratic style of education remained.

Beyond the rigidity and uniformity of the factory became a theme in much of the writing during this period. Henry Cope, the general secretary of the REA argued that in the period from 1870 to 1908, the Sunday school was controlled by a factory understanding. He wrote, "The insistent confining of the teaching work of

the school to the rigid lines of mechanical, business
uniformity seriously retarded its educational development. The school has never been successfully conducted
on the plan of a factory."[12] Cope felt that the church
had finally understood that the school of the church
was a "definite teaching agency." For a model, he
advocated the emerging professional corporation model
of the public school.

Further evidence for this change can be seen in the
way the word efficiency, which predominated public education after 1911, also predominated church education.
For example, the title for the standards developed by
the Sunday School Council was changed in 1914 to Standard of Efficiency. The concern of public education
for efficiency was transferred to the church school.[13]
Also efficiency came to be used in titles and chapters
of many church education texts. Cope's Efficiency in
the Sunday School published in 1912 is one example.[14]

Three complementary ideas gained acceptance in the
second decade of the twentieth century as means of
shifting the model for the church school to a corporate
model: (a) the advocacy of a local church committee on
education, (b) the development of a national system of
religious education, and (c) acceptance of the idea of
a profession of religious educators.

The notion of a committee on education in the congregation to be a responsible policy-making body of the
church's educational work was written into the 1913
standards set by the REA. Drawing from public school
practice, it was argued that the church should have an
education committee which would serve the church school
in the same way that the school board did the public
school. Its job primarily was to survey educational
needs, adopt curricula, select teachers, supervise the
total educational program, and select a Director of
Religious Education, trained in religious pedagogy,
who would then supervise and direct the church school
and train teachers. This director or "teaching pastor"
of the church was to function like a principal or
superintendent of schools.[15] Note that the education
work of the church was extended beyond the Sunday
morning time and placed under the strict control of the
church governing board. The standards further suggested
other administrative personnel, from librarian to
secretary, that the church school would need.

Drawing from the research and conversation reflected in these REA standards, Walter Athearn published in
1914 The Church School as a definitive attempt to apply
to the church the ". . . scientific research that has
done so much to increase the efficiency of secular education."[16] He highlighted the role of the education
committee to survey, supervise and coordinate the work
of the various agencies of education within the church--
to provide a "central, intelligent system" for the
church's program. Church education theorists hoped that
this committee would consist of persons familiar with
education theory and capable of functioning as a corporation board of directors to employ a professional to
carry out its wishes.

        Secondly, a national system of religious edu-
cation was a logical extension of the notion of coordination in the local parish. Progressive church educators saw a need, again parallel to the public school,
to provide a means of coordinating local church programs
into area-wide and denominational programing, and ultimately into a national program. It was hoped that the
local, state and national public education structures
could be matched. Athearn was again a leader in the
propagation of this notion describing it in Religious
Education and American Democracy in 1917. By the time
of the creation of the International Council in 1922,
his notion was accepted as a primary agenda. Athearn
argued that a unified system of American education demanded ". . . the establishing of a system of church
schools which will parallel the public schools all the
way from kindergarten to the university. These two
systems of schools must be closely coordinated in the
interest of a unified educational program, which will
guarantee to every child both intelligence and godli-
ness."[17] To begin to build the efficient system he
argued that demonstration models must be initiated in
communities and competent religious educators must be
trained.[18]

        Documents of the three major religious education
groups reflect the support for this idea.[19] It provided a means for religious educators to learn from the
public school and to demonstrate to public school educators the quality of their educational reflection. The
creation of the International Council itself was seen
as the coordinating structure to effect such a national,
parallel program of religious instruction. Through it
denominational, interdenominational, and extra-church

organizations were to relate to encourage coorelation and to upgrade educational quality.[20]

Thirdly, the complex design demanded educational professionals as competent in religious education as were public school educators. The director was seen as a person who was both called by God for a particular ministry and a professional in Christian education as skillful as teachers, lawyers, and doctors. Therefore, in the director, religious devotion and educational expertise were to be combined.

Great expectations were placed on the director. He or she was to be the pivotal person in the realization of the grand purpose of church education. Church leaders were therefore particularly concerned that standards be set to define the profession and to enhance educational requirements. In each of the three major religious education organizations, local church teachers, directors, professors, and denominational executives could learn and share educational processes and innovations. For example, in the International Council a group was developed to be concerned with assisting directors in the promotion and development of their profession.[21] Particular attention was given to how colleges, seminaries, and communities could develop more effective educational programs for directors.[22] The concern was to prepare church teachers and administrators who were as competent as were their public school counterparts and as well educated as clergy. Commitment and devotion were thought to be important, but they were not sufficient. Education and expertise needed to be added.

The duties also set directors apart from Sunday school leaders of the previous era. While these new professionals were expected to teach, as was true in the earlier era, the director was to be responsible for communicating the importance of religious education in both community and church, and to inspire coordination within church programming and among the efforts of various churches and the public schools. Therefore, the director was primarily a supervisor, administrator, or coordinator paralleling more directly the public school superintendent.

So much hope was put into the director that the descriptions were quite expansive. One example is from George Webb, the secretary of the Educational Council of the Evangelical Churches. He wrote:

The director is more than a teacher, more than an organizer. He is a prophet, a seer, an inspirer in fields of education and of religion until both become one in religious education. He should be of virile, red blooded Christian manhood, with great faith in humanity and instructive ability to recognize the best in men and to see that childhood and youth hold the larger promise. He should be cheerful, optimistic, patient, clean, square, true to self and fellows and to truth.[23]

While this description sounds much like the "Boy Scout Oath," it does exhibit the hope leaders expressed. In the professional director local church and national work were to be focused. With a director who knew how to coordinate the church and the community, and with a national professional network for support and education, church education leaders thought that the church school could finally be created.

A corporate model became the model for the church's school. To see more clearly the changes and continuities which resulted in this period of the transformation from a factory to a corporate conception, the responses of church education leaders to particular issues of method of instruction, pupil classification, buildings, and teacher training need to be examined. Each of these issues had also been important in the earlier period.[24]

No issue dominated the early progressive period (1890-1910) as much as that of graded curriculum. Church leaders felt that graded instruction provided a new method of instruction. Since the 1870s Sunday schools had been classified by age levels, where each age-level class was to study the same lesson drawn from the uniform lesson series. Yet research in childhood development which came to predominate in the public school, as well as the practical difficulty that many qualified church nursery teachers felt in teaching the uniform lesson, led to lobbying for a thoroughly graded series.

As early as 1893 the International Lesson Committee felt it had to respond to criticisms of the uniform lesson series by primary workers. While noting that the committee had to decide whether a primary series was possible, its executive, Warren Randolph defended the uniform series by arguing that it had encouraged

the study of scripture, had improved the quality of
instruction, and had made the training of teachers
easier.[25] From here on until the end of the first decade of the twentieth century the church education world
was filled with controversy over the merits of graded
instruction. Those who defended the lessons feared
the loss of uniformity and those who challenged feared
the loss of pupils through inadequate methods. No
issue so divided the Christian educators until the
fundamentalist/modernist controversies of the late 1920s
and 1930s. In fact the difficulty in getting graded
lessons accepted was in part responsible for the creation of the REA and the Sunday School Council of
Evangelical Denominations.

    Within Sunday school organizations themselves, the
International Primary Union which had been founded in
1870 led the way to graded curricula. Initially the
union supported the uniform lesson as useful in helping
organize training sessions for teachers, but through
their child-study clubs, leaders of the union discovered
that the lesson had to be adapted to the young child
and that graded instruction was the only means to do
so.[26]

    The supporters of grading did not challenge the
past effectiveness of the uniform lesson. In fact they
praised it because it had upgraded the church's school,
but they argued that it was not sufficient for a new
day. People learn best, they argued, when content,
instruction, and life are coordinated.

    After the founding of the REA in 1903, the cause
of grading had another powerful ally. The first
issues of Religious Education include several articles
on developmental psychology and religious knowledge,
and its leadership recommended books on graded Sunday
schools--one of which was Samuel Haslett's The Pedagogical Bible School.[27] Haslett wrote that the way
to increase efficiency in the Sunday school was to improve the content of teaching. While organization,
equipment, time, libraries, and teachers all needed to
be improved, he argued that curriculum was pivotal;
therefore, he used contemporary psychological research
to outline the developmental processes for a scheme of
lessons.[28]

    The International Lesson Committee did respond to
the push for graded material, but it did so reluctantly

110

and in concert with a defense of the uniform lessons.
The committee members, many of whom had served for over
twenty years, thought that the issue of instruction had
been decided in 1872 and were reluctant to reopen it,
but by 1899 an International Primary Course was initiated.[29] With continual pressure in 1908 the association
recommended the development of a totally graded curriculum to supplement the uniform series, which by 1911
was credited with inspiring "phenomenal growth" in
some schools, so that in 1914 a second graded series,
simpler for smaller churches, was begun as was one
recognizing adolescent religious development.[30] Grading
thus became the means that progressive church educators
used to solve the problem of method of instruction.
Grading set the framework for pupil classification,
building construction, and teacher training.

By 1913 the REA recommended a form of classification which was in 1916 to be adopted and expanded by
the Joint Committee on Standards created by the Sunday
School Council and the International Sunday School
Association. The following age classification was
recommended: (a) Cradle Roll Department, (b) Beginner
Department (ages 4-5), (c) Primary Department (ages
6-8), (d) Junior Department (ages 9-12), (e) Intermediate Department (ages 13-16), (f) Senior Department
(ages 17-20), and (g) Adult Department.[31] In the next
year the youth subcommittee of the Joint Committee further refined its work into three groups respectively
ages 13-14, 15-17, and 18-24.[32]

The standards for each age classification listed
knowledge and behavior aims for religious education at
this age level and means to effect these aims. The
standards were comprehensive. For example, the standard for the Beginners Department listed the following
conduct goals for children four and five years old:

1. Love, trust and reverence for God
2. Association of the Heavenly Father with daily
   life
3. Right behavior
4. Love for God through prayer, praise, and effort
   to please Him
5. Love for others through acts of helpfulness.[33]

The standard further listed content to be developed in
the curriculum, the design of a home-like learning
environment appropriate for these children, methods to
stimulate children's self-expression, and standards

for teachers. The standards therefore sought to provide a comprehensive plan for nurturing children through stages of religious development that would lead them to make a commitment for Jesus Christ in the Junior Department and gradually grow into full participation and leadership in the life of the church.

With the new organization, new "graded" buildings modeled on the public school were essential.[34] They were part of the means of instruction. Several had been constructed by 1913 which modeled directly on the public school. They demonstrated that the old Akron plan auditorium was totally inappropriate. The ideal was that each church would build an educational building as attractive and functional as the public school building, with ample lighting; ventilation; sound-proof walls; an abundance of maps, chairs and pictures; manual-work materials; and musical instruments.

A comprehensive survey of potential styles for Sunday school buildings was conducted by the Sunday School Council. Its Committee on Church and Sunday-School Buildings reluctantly admitted that much church and Sunday school construction had been haphazard and unthinking. They argued that since space has an effect on the program, a graded Sunday school needed a graded building.[35] The new building plans consisted of individual classrooms for small groups of children and adults divided by ages, and in larger churches, assembly rooms for departments were also to be constructed. In addition, each school was to provide special rooms for superintendent, secretary, maps, and even a mothers' lounge. The new designs sought to embody the church school in a facility which was ordered, graded, and formed as the best public schools.

Graded classes also stimulated greater interest in teacher training. A higher quality teacher was thought to be needed, but the task of the teacher was thought to be easier because a teacher could now deal directly with the needs of the children. Teacher training was taken seriously. The International Sunday School Association set in 1905 as a goal that every church school teacher be trained, in 1912 the Teacher Training Commission of the REA published its standards, in 1915 the Sunday School Council prepared teacher training standards which were also adopted by the International Association, and by 1919 the Sunday School Council initiated a national teacher training drive to encourage instructional preparation for all teachers.[36]

The courses of training developed in the standards were quite ambitious. In the REA standard, two years of elementary study were outlined. It assumed the Biblical training of Sunday school in childhood was sufficient so that the first-year course could concentrate specifically on the nature of the child, pedagogical method, and classroom management. It included forty hours of classroom study on child development in the age-group of specialization, on content of the faith, on principles and application of pedagogy, and on educational organization, combined with twenty-six hours of supervised classroom practice work of observing, assisting, or substituting.[37] These courses required the development of teacher reference libraries and the establishment of city-wide Sunday school teacher-training institutes, but they "guaranteed" teachers prepared as competently as in the public school.

The concern for teacher training further led to the development of national training schools. The International Sunday School Association established at Lake Geneva in Wisconsin in 1912 the Training School for Sunday School Leadership. This school offered a four-year course of study to prepare leaders and short-term courses to increase the competence of present Sunday school teachers. Increasingly colleges and seminaries also developed courses of study in church school work.[38] The church's normal work did seem to flourish in the second decade of the twentieth century with the search for ways to enhance the competence of hundreds of thousands of Sunday school officers and teachers. Most of its leaders were motivated by the vision of a Sunday school that rivaled the public school with better trained teachers and superintendents operating the most efficient educational institutions.

An ideal of the public school definitely served as a model for church school leaders to emulate. In the 1910s the theories of the religious education leadership demanded that a good church school would be well organized, directed by trained leadership, staffed with trained teachers using graded curricula, and situated in a modern educational facility. One further step toward a corporate-style bureaucratic school was taken when most denominations fully accepted the responsibility of directing their churches' educational programs. National denominational commissions of education prepared standardized curricula and training courses to be used throughout the churches and sent educational consultants to oversee and upgrade work in local churches.[39]

113

Through these innovations the Sunday school was transformed into a church school. Church school leaders hoped the very important work of educating the nation in religion and morals, which could not be done in the mismanaged assembly hall of the old Sunday school, could now be done in the school of the church. The effectiveness of each school was measured by its approximation to the school model. While the details of the structure of the old Sunday school had changed, the basic commitment of Protestant Christian education to a form in relation to the public school was unchanged. The church school had a glorious future, it was thought, because its form was improved--classified, graded, and organized like the public school.

The Scope of the Church School

When the Sunday school became an important part of the church's ministry in the latter fourth of the nineteenth century, pastors and Sunday school leaders had to address how the Sunday school related to various ministries of the church. Sunday school leaders of that time argued that the Sunday school was only one of the church's agencies which carried educational ministry. They felt the work of the Sunday school needed to be unified within the church's ministry. The family, the pulpit, and church life all had educational responsibilities. These leaders knew that the Sunday school could not carry the educational ministry alone; therefore, a broader scope for Christian education was defined. The church was to be the focus, but in it, family, pulpit, Sunday school, and fellowship life, as well as the agencies of public religious education, were to be coordinated.

The scope of the Sunday school in this early period was further defined by the configuration of institutions supportive of Christian education. As Robert Lynn has demonstrated, there had been an ecology of educational institutions supportive of the content and message of mainline Protestantism. The content of the culture expressed in public school and voluntary reform agencies was supportive of the content expressed in the church, particularly through its Sunday school.[40] While this ecology was in place through the latter part of the nineteenth century, the message of the Sunday school found cultural support. It functioned as one element in a larger educational context. However, by the turn of the century and into the first decades of the

114

twentieth century, with increased cultural pluralism, this ecology began to deteriorate. Church education leaders had to be more intentional about the means to carry out Christian education. Their re-definition of scope built on the conviction that society, family, pulpit and Sunday school had worked together in the midst of the past ecology, but the re-definition went beyond this ecology to suggest that the church, rather than the culture, should serve as the unifying factor. They seem to have felt that by will the church could replace the educational configuration of the earlier period. They asked: if the church does not accept this responsibility, who will?

The definition of the church school itself, with its education council that was to coordinate agencies of Christian education and with its relation to a national system of church education, represented an attempt to provide a new configuration for Protestant education. Also the formation of the Sunday School Council of Evangelical Denominations was even traced by several leaders to the very problem of correlating the agencies of the church with the Sunday school.[41] The lack of organization and unity was thought to mute the effectiveness of the church's education. Walter Athearn argued that while one-half of church members might be influenced by the Sunday school, another one-fourth was only influenced by the other "educational" agencies in the church, that is young people's societies, men and women's organizations, and junior societies, to name a few. He argued that the lack of unity and the overlap drained energy and blunted the effect that any one agency could have. Seeing the overlap as inefficient he argued that the problem of church education would in great part be solved by a "central, intelligent system."[42] His notions were supported and expanded.

A further example of this conviction can be drawn from the research of Wilhelmina Stooker, a children's worker in New York. In attempting to assess how well the children's standards of the Sunday School Council were being used and how effective they were, she concluded with disappointment that the lack of coordination muted the potential influence of the standards. She wrote that her research had ". . . revealed the impossibility of giving the child a well rounded religious education without securing adequate . . . cooperation among the overhead controlling bodies of all organizations that have to do with religious education of children."[43] Therefore, attempts were made to

115

recognize the scope of Christian education agencies and
to coordinate them on the local and community level.

The formula for local level coordination built
heavily on the nineteenth-century definition of scope.
The home, congregational life, worship, and the church's
school program were to be brought into relationship with
each other. The director and education committee were
to be made responsible for the correlation. To quote
Athearn, the church school was to be ". . . as comprehensive as the church itself."[44] The message of one
agency was to complement the message of another.

The unity of the agencies within the church came
to be symbolized in the theological and educational
image of a religious community of learning. Many church
educators argued that the church's education was more
than a schooling approach, rather persons were thought
to learn the faith as they participated in the religious
community or congregation. William Clayton Bower was
one of the leaders who expressed this ideal. He argued
that the person learned to be a Christian by practicing
the faith.

> The church that would educate its young in religion
> must organize itself as a religious community.
> Religious education is vastly more than religious
> instruction. It is at bottom a sharing of reli-
> gious experience in a community dominated by
> religious ideals and motives and absorbed in
> carrying out the projects of the kingdom of God.[45]

Therefore, a central task of the church educator was to
organize the church into a religious community and tap
its potential. Bower also reminded educators that the
whole community educated--the schools, the press, the
moving pictures, etc.[46] Therefore, the moral and religious tone of the community had a profound effect on
religious education. If the church was to have an impact, he argued, it needed to become a religious community which reached out to affect the character of
the social community. The church's education could not
be effective without influencing its social and cultural context.

Consequently, church educators looked beyond the
church, seeking to build a community program of religious education. The first place to start was to coordinate a local church program with that of other
churches and religious volunteer agencies in the

community.[47] Such coordination was to allow the religious forces to have a more unified front and to provide them with enough power to seek to affect community
agencies. Such a community strategy would enable the
churches to research the impact and needs of the community and to respond appropriately with instructional,
training, recreational, and action programs.[48] One
essential part of such a program was to be weekday
religious schools.[49] Church educators experimented
with a variety of strategies from credit school courses
offered in churches to released-time activities, but
they were convinced that the church's education had to
affect directly the public school. They were all in
agreement that an effective Christian education program had to be broadened beyond the church to include
the other learning arenas of persons' lives. It was
hoped that a system of church schools, community
training schools, vacation church schools, weekday religious schools, and community outreach could be created
to respond to the wider learning environment. To build
Christian character required strategies beyond the
Sunday school. The scope of the Sunday school was
broadened to include the character of the religious
community and the influence of its outreach.

Change and Continuity in the Church School

The church school was a transformed institution!
In many respects it was significantly different from the
Sunday school. The form had been made more complex, its
administration was more grandiose, its building was
more modern, and it was administered by a new professional, the director of religious education. Even some
public school and progressive educators came to judge
some church schools as excellent schools. For example,
Eugene Exman, a progressive educator, analyzed the work
at several model church schools like the ones at River-
side Church in New York and Hyde Park Baptist Church in
Chicago. Exman commented that these schools were two
examples

. . . of the church schools that are applying the
most up-to-date educational methods to character
training. . . . They represent a new attitude on
the part of church teachers, substituting trained
teachers and attractive courses for rally days and
class pins. In objective they have much in common
with the old-time Sunday school. Their aim is to
put religion to work to make it contribute to day

117

by day living. It is in method that they differ
using project as well as precept and weaving
religion into the fabric of common experience.[50]

In several places the dream of church school educators
that their school would be taken seriously as an educational program began to be reached.

However, despite these numerous changes, the
church school remained in significant continuity with
its past. The three central issues of purpose, form,
and scope continued and their solutions were clearly
built on foundations of the past. In terms of purpose
Christian character was to be the result of the church's
educational program. The Sunday school was not seen as
much as an adjunct of the revival, but the process of
developmentally-based education was to achieve the
same result. Marion Lawrance, the General Secretary
for the International Sunday School Association from
1899-1922, continued to remind church school leaders
that their task was to reform the school in such a way
as to continue to save souls for God. As he called to
make the Sunday school efficient, he also warned: "Let
us not get tangled up in the machinery of our organization and forget that immortal souls are perishing
every day all about us."[51] Such an agenda continued
to avoid other implications of its definition of purpose: to what degree was the church school concerned
with theological knowledge, what was the relationship
of theological knowledge to Christian character, and
what was the appropriate role of the church in relation to culture--was it to ignore culture, transform
it, or celebrate it? All of these implications were
worked at in various ways without an intentional
theological analysis; therefore, several religious educators moved in the 1920s and 1930s to character study
alone and some neo-orthodox critics of the 1930s and
1940s seemed to ignore character in favor of knowledge.

The form of the church school increasingly became
defined as both of the church and of the school. The
Protestant strategy formed in the mid-1800s to build a
school of the church continued. Curriculum, method of
instruction, teacher training, and building style were
all transformed during the period as well as church
school administration made more professional. Nevertheless, church educators had to continue to struggle
to integrate the church school into the life of the
church. Its new and separate buildings were almost
a metaphor of its relation to the church as a vibrant,

118

significant <u>adjunct</u> to the ministry of the church. The church school retained a separate identity. It was a program of the church, but only marginally connected to the church. A few educators saw how to influence the educative character of church life. But most attempted to administratively and bureaucratically coordinate programs and content, rather than building the educative community of which they talked.

Finally, in terms of scope, most educators realized, as they always had, that the church school could not carry the educational responsibility by itself. The church school was one institution in a much broader matrix to influence persons and culture. Church educators attempted to solve this dilemma by creating a church school system parallel to the public school. They dreamed of a national bureaucratic structure to coordinate church education. Yet the actual manner in which this system was to substitute for a cultural ecology and the actual success of its attempts can seriously be questioned.

Change and continuity both explain the development of the Sunday school in the early twentieth century. The experience of transformation led progressive educators to celebrate the swiftness with which their changes were accepted. Yet these same progressives ignored that many of their changes were simply rewriting of past experience in new language. A sense of change, it seems, causes church educators to ignore underlying consensus and structure. It is that consensus and structure which must be addressed.

Notes

[1]Report of Committee on Education of the International Sunday School Council of Religious Education, by Walter S. Athearn, Chairman (Kansas City: International Sunday School Council of Religious Education, 1922), pp. 6-7.

[2]Ibid., p. 11.

[3]Hugh S. Mcgill, "A Comprehensive Program of Education, Secular and Religious," in International Sunday School Association, Organized Sunday School Work, 1918-1922, Official Report of the Sixteenth International Sunday School Convention, ed. Herbert H. Smith (Chicago: The International Sunday School Council of Religious Education, 1922), p. 162.

[4]See Ibid.; Walter Athearn, "The Outlook for Christian Education," in Organized Sunday School Work, 1918-1922, pp. 164-179; and Report of Committee on Education.

[5]See as an example the conversation of William Clayton Bower, H. Shelton Smith and Henry P. Van Dusen in "Issues in Religious Education," Religion in Life 7 (Winter 1942-43):31-52.

[6]William R. Funk, "Report of the President," in Sunday School Council of Evangelical Denominations, Minutes, Third Annual Meeting (New York: Office of the Secretary, 1913), p. 19.

[7]B. S. Winchester, "The Next Things in Religious Education," in International Sunday School Association, Organized Sunday School Work in America, 1908-1911, Official Report of the Thirteenth International Sunday School Convention (Chicago: International Sunday School Association, 1911), pp. 327-329.

[8]"The Church School: Report of the Committee on the 'Correlation of Educational Agencies of the Local Church'," by Walter S. Athearn, Chm., Religious Education 8 (April 1913):32.

[9]Athearn, "Church School," p. 32.

[10]See for example Report of Committee on Education, pp. 11-12; Winchester, "Next Things in Religious Education," pp. 327-329; and William Clayton Bower, The Educational Task of the Local Church (St. Louis: Teacher Training Publishing Association, 1921), pp. 7-29.

[11]See for example George Albert Coe, The Core of Good Teaching: A Sunday-School Curriculum, Completely Graded Series (New York: Charles Scribner's Sons, 1911).

[12] Henry F. Cope, The Evolution of the Sunday School (Boston: Pilgrim Press, 1911), p. 108. See also Henry H. Meyer, "The Harvest Vision and the Opportunity of the Sunday School," in International Sunday School Association, Organized Sunday School Work in America, 1911-1914, Official Report of the Fourteenth International Convention (Chicago: International Sunday School Association, 1914), p. 463.

[13] "Report of the Educational and Extension Section," in Sunday School Council of Evangelical Denominations, Minutes, Fourth Annual Meeting (Philadelphia: Office of the Secretary, 1914), p. 61.

[14] Henry F. Cope, Efficiency in the Sunday School (New York: George N. Doran Co., 1912). See also the use of efficiency in Walter Athearn, The Church School, p. viii; William Clayton Bower, The Educational Task of the Local Church, pp. 14-17; and Ernest J. Denner, The Sunday School Under Scientific Management (Milwaukee: Young Churchman, 1914).

[15] Athearn, "Church School," pp. 34-36. See also "Sunday School Standards: Illustrations of Advance Ideals in the Ten-Point Plan," Religious Education 8 (June 1913):231-234.

[16] Walter Athearn, The Church School (Boston: Pilgrim Press, 1914), p. viii. This same style is reflected in the work of most church educators in this day. See also Henry Cope Modern Sunday School and Its Present Day Task (New York: Fleming H. Revell Co., 1907-1916).

[17] Walter Athearn, Religious Education and American Democracy (Boston: Pilgrim Press, 1917), p. 21. See all of chapter one for a description of this system, pp. 2-21.

[18] Ibid., p. 21.

[19] For example see Lester Bradner, "President's Opening Address: A National Programme in Religious Education," in Sunday School Council of Evangelical Denominations, Minutes, Ninth Annual Meeting (New York: George T. Webb, Secretary, 1919), pp. 12-20. Such a notion was officially adopted in 1918. For a description of the adoption and addresses in its favor see International Sunday School Association, Organized Sunday School Work in North America, 1914-1918, Official Report of the Fifteenth International Sunday School Association Convention, ed. Herbert Smith (Chicago: International Sunday School Association, 1918), pp. 94-112.

[20] Report of Committee on Education, pp. 36-37.

[21] Ibid., p. 15.

[22] See for example Ibid., pp. 38-43; and A. Ducan Yocum, "Correlation of Departments of Education and Religious Education in Colleges and Universities," in Organized Sunday School Work in North America, 1918-1922, pp. 454-462.

[23] "Local Directors of Religious Education," in Organized Sunday School Work in North America, 1918-1922, p. 464.

[24] See Chapter II section on Form.

[25] Warren Randolph, "The Seventh Triennial Report of the International Lesson Committee," in Seventh International and World's Second Sunday School Conventions (Chicago: Executive Council of International Sunday School Convention, 1893), pp. 168-182. See also the criticism of the uniform lessons in the same volume in Mrs. M. G. Kennedy, "International Lessons in the Primary Class," pp. 256-264.

[26] Mrs. J. W. Barnes, "The Work of the Primary Union," in The Eighth International Sunday School Convention (Chicago: Executive Committee, 1896), pp. 221-223.

[27] The names of Bagley and Starbuck are two examples. See for example W. C. Bagley, "The Pegagogy of Morality and Religion as Related to the Periods of Development," Religious Education 4 (April 1909):91-106. Also several churches who had developed graded material are also highlighted. See "Sunday School Curricula Outlines," Religious Education 2 (December 1907):170-188. For the recommendation of books on graded instruction see Cope, Evolution of the Sunday School, p. 145. See also Samuel B. Haslett, The Pedagogical Bible School: A Scientific Study of the Sunday School with Chief Reference to the Curriculum, 3rd ed. (New York: Fleming H. Revell Co., 1903).

[28] Haslett, Pedagogical Bible School, pp. 340-341.

[29] A. E. Dunning, "Report of the Lesson Committee," in Ninth International Sunday School Convention (Chicago: Executive Committee, 1899), pp. 51-52.

[30]William N. Hartshorne, "A Survey of Sunday-School Work in North America," in World's Sunday School Association, World-Wide Sunday-School Work: The Official Report of the World's Sixth Sunday-School Convention, ed. William N. Hartshorne (Chicago: The Executive Committee of the World's Sunday School Association, 1910), p. 196; Mary Foster Bryner, "Report of the Elementary Department," in Organized Sunday School Work in America, 1908-1911, p. 209; and Marion Lawrance, "Report of the General Secretary," and John L. Alexander, "Secondary Division Report," in Organized Sunday School Work in America, 1911-1914, pp. 124-185.

[31]Athearn, "Church School," pp. 37-46; and "Educational and Extension Section," in Sunday School Council of Evangelical Denominations, Minutes, Sixth Annual Meeting (Philadelphia: George T. Webb, Secretary, 1916), pp. 37-57.

[32]"Educational and Extension Section," in Sunday School Council of Evangelical Denominations, Minutes, Seventh Annual Meeting (Philadelphia: George T. Webb, Secretary, 1917), pp. 44-48.

[33]"Educational and Extension Section," Minutes, Sixth Annual Meeting, p. 40.

[34]Athearn, "Church School," p. 46. See also Mary Foster Bryner, "Report of the Superintendent--The Elementary Division," in Organized Sunday School Work in America, 1911-1914, pp. 146-147; Henry F. Cope, "Ten Years' Progress in Religious Education," Religious Education 8 (June 1913):126; and Henry H. Meyer, "The Harvest Vision and the Opportunity of the Sunday School," in Organized Sunday School Work in America, 1911-1914, p. 464.

[35]"Report of Committee on Church and Sunday-School Buildings," in Sunday School Council of Evangelical Denominations, Minutes, Ninth Annual Meeting (New York: George T. Webb, Secretary, 1919), p. 89.

[36]H. M. Hamill, "Teacher-Training Department," in World-Wide Sunday School Work, p. 393; "Teacher Training Commission of the Religious Education Association: Report of the Committee on Elementary and Advanced Teacher-Training Courses for Sunday Schools," by Walter S. Athearn, Chm, Religious Education 7 (April 1912):81-87; "Report of the Education and Extension Section," in Sunday School Council of Evangelical Denominations, Minutes, Fifth Annual Meeting (Philadelphia: George T. Webb, Secretary, 1915), pp. 32-34; and "Report of Teacher Training Drive Committee," in Minutes Ninth Annual Meeting, pp. 67-76.

[37]Athearn, "Teacher Training Commission," pp. 82-84; and Mrs. J. W. Barnes, "Report for Committee on Teacher Training Courses for Special Departments," Religious Education 7 (April 1912):94-95.

[38]Lawrance, "Report of the General Secretary," p. 115; and Cope, "Ten Years Progress in Religious Education," pp. 137-143.

[39]For an interesting description of this development see Robert Lynn and Elliott Wright, The Big Little School: Sunday Child of American Protestantism (New York: Harper & Row, 1971), pp. 77-99.

[40]Robert W. Lynn, "The Last of the Great Religious Movements," The Duke Divinity School Review 40 (Fall 1975):153.

[41]George T. Webb, "Report of the Secretary," in Minutes, Seventh Annual Meeting, pp. 23-24.

[42]Athearn, Church School, pp. 13-16, 22-23.

[43]Wilhelmina Stooker, "Sunday Sessions and Related Activities-- Children's Work," in Sunday School Council of Evangelical Denominations, Papers and Addresses Given at Eleventh Annual Meeting (Toronto: Council Office, 1921), p. 63.

[44]Athearn, Church School, p. 1.

[45]See Bower, Educational Task of Local Church, pp. 42-43.

[46]Ibid., pp. 93-94.

[47]"Local Directors of Religious Education," in Organized Sunday School Work in North America, 1918-1922, p. 464.

[48]See Frank M. Sheldon, "The Essential Elements in a Community Program of Religious Education," and George Platt Knox, "The Organization of a Community for a Program of Religious Education," in Papers and Addresses, pp. 17-27.

[49]For an example of models, see Henry H. Meyer, "Report of the Secretary," in Minutes, Fourth Annual Meeting, p. 29; and "Committee on Religious Education and the Public Schools," in Minutes, Seventh Annual Meeting, pp. 56-62.

[50]Eugene Exman, "Sunday Schools Have Changed Too," School and Society 47 (June 11, 1938):765-766.

[51]Marion Lawrance, "Report of the General Secretary," in International Sunday School Association, Organized Sunday-School Work in America, 1905-1908: Official Report of the Twelfth International Convention (Chicago: International Sunday School Association, 1908), p. 157.

126

CHAPTER VI

THE PROGRESSIVE CHURCH SCHOOL

The first three decades of the twentieth century were indeed a period of enthusiasm and change in Protestant church education. Those involved defined this period as one of the most expansive and fruitful in the history of Protestant churches' concerns for education. Two of the most powerful spokespersons for the progressive church school during this period were Henry Frederick Cope and George Albert Coe. The career of both is coextensive with the period of greatest expansion and transformation. Correspondingly both were credited as primary agents in the transformation of church education. Their involvement thus is an illustration of the progressive church school in action. Its excesses, its contributions, and its difficulties are apparent in their work.

Cope and Coe were major architects of the progressive spirit in Protestant church education. From his position as General Secretary for the Religious Education Association (REA), Henry Cope focused the variety of research and writing efforts in religious education into a unified program. In fact, his own writing is a summary of the best of the thinking in religious education. Through it, he popularized the new ideas and made them accessible to pastors, educators, and the laity. He saw his task as agent of REA to provide a "think tank" free of denominational and administrative agendas and capable of transcending conventional practice in order to ". . . think and investigate and speak fundamentally and freely . . ." about the nature and potential of religious education.[1]

George Albert Coe was the primary academic spokesperson for progressive religious education. From his academic positions at Northwestern University, Union Theological Seminary, and Teachers College in New York City, as well as through his service as officer in REA, Coe sought to integrate modern educational theory, psychological research, and religious study into a unified approach to the transformation of the American character. He was called by his contemporaries both a pioneer and prophet for the reconstruction of religion and education.[2]

Both Cope and Coe were staunch supporters of the reform movement in Protestant education. They believed

that the progressive church school had provided the
church with the real potential to be the church in mission to the culture. Both were concerned to see the
church's education on a par with and related to the
public educational system, and both recognized that
education was much broader than the school. The difference between the two is that Cope was the popularizer, representing and unifying progressive church
education theory, while Coe was the theorist who analyzed issues in depth.

Cope was very optimistic about the church's ability
to provide a comprehensive program of religious education for the culture. This theme is most successfully
developed in a book which was published posthumously,
Organizing the Church School: A Comprehensive Scheme
for Religious Educational Activities for Children and
Youth. Here he tried to develop how the church was a
social system which taught the faith throughout its
whole life. He believed that if the church did not
become such an educational system that religious education would neither be taught nor learned.[3]

Coe, on the other hand, emphasized the importance
of the church, but he also argued that the church was
more a captive of culture than a transformer of culture. He advocated a transformation of the church itself so that it could transform life. Education was an
experience in all of life and therefore religious education had to transcend the church to affect all life.
The distinction between secular and religious education
increasingly became for him a false distinction and he
was frustrated by conversations which did not consider
the nature of the church itself.[4] Coe moved from church
education to a concern for the education of the
public. The contrasts between these two illustrate the
dynamics at work in progressive church education.

Progressive religious education itself was in deep
trouble by 1930. The movement which had infused so
much excitement into the church and educational ministries seemed to lose its direction, nerve, and vitality.
Adelaide Case, who taught at Teachers College in the
1920s and 1930s, argued in her analysis of progressive
religious education that the movement almost came to a
complete stop with the depression.[5] She further argued
that it "failed" because the depression dried up the
funds needed to expand the new profession of religious
education and that the liberal, optimistic theology of
the progressive church school was not sufficient to meet

128

the theological and meaning challenge posed by the depression and World War II.6 Her analysis is indeed plausible, for while much writing was done during the 1930s and 1940s on liberal or progressive religious education, most of it was defensive and attempted to re-establish a previous position rather than to continue to develop it. It is indeed interesting to note that this movement which had attempted to unify religious education and American democracy lost its prophetic voice and ability to speak meaningfully to that culture in deterioration.

In the contrast of Cope and Coe the seeds for this failure may be apparent. As Coe would argue, it was not enough for the church to respond to culture, rather both the culture and the church needed to be transformed. Of course Coe was hurt by the demise of progressive education, but the biggest pain came from the failure of religious education to address adequately, constructively, and practically human life and culture. For Coe theology had to be practical, seeking the transformation of life.

The Influence of Cope and Coe

During his lifetime Henry Frederick Cope was awarded three honorary degrees for his service to and leadership in education.7 These honors symbolize that he was recognized as one of the best of the progressive church educators. Cope was born in England where he attended elementary school and worked in industry and the military before becoming a lay evangelist in the Baptist Church. In 1891 Cope emigrated to the United States for a theological education at the Southern Baptist Theological Seminary in Louisville, Kentucky. After two years of study, and before completing his degree, he left seminary to be ordained. From 1893 to 1903 he served two parishes in New York, one in Illinois, and one in Montana, during which time he became recognized for his concern for more adequate methods of Bible study and wrote a book which recorded his experiences with the "Bonanza Bible Class." Therefore, when in 1903 the organizers of the REA sought to involve representatives from all over the country, Cope was invited to come to Chicago as the representative from Montana.

Not only did Cope accept the invitation, but he moved his family to Chicago where he began to write and

lecture extensively. In 1905 he agreed to be assistant
secretary for the REA. Following then a period as
acting secretary when he began to put the REA on solid
financial footing, in 1907 he became General Secretary
serving until his death at fifty-three in August of
1923. As General Secretary Cope made his significant
contribution to religious education. He translated the
enthusiasm of those interested in reforming religious
education into practical reality by financially stabi-
lizing REA and by providing it with an organizational
structure to contribute to research in religious education. He defined it as a research and development
organization which while not competing with denominational or inter-denominational religious education
agencies in producing curriculum materials and program
materials provided those agencies with the intellectual
stimulation to reform and upgrade curricula and programs.[8] Also as General Secretary he edited over 100
issues of Religious Education, the journal which became a major forum for reform and intellectual reflection on religious education.

While Cope was not an original thinker in the
field of religious education, he was an expert organizer and popularizer, writing profusely to summarize the
new ideas in discipline, and he was an effective editor
encouraging the original contributions of others. In
fact his The Modern Sunday School in Principle and
Practice published in 1907 was recommended as the most
adequate statement of Sunday school theory for its
time.[9] Also in his history of the Sunday school movement, The Evolution of the Sunday School, published in
1911, and in his ten year reports on the progress in
religious education, he was to define for others the
crucial events in the development of the church's education. He therefore served as "weather vane" and
interpreter defining for other religious educators what
was important for the field.[10]

Theodore Soares at the time of Cope's death summarized his influence in the following manner:

> His position was unique. It was not that of the
> original scientific thinker in this new field,
> although he shared the scientific spirit and
> worked out his own principles with remarkable
> independence of judgment. It was not that of the
> investigator, actually initiating experiments and
> discovering truth, though he was keenly alive to
> the importance of research and was leading the

Association in later years with great earnestness into this field. It was not that of organizing religious education programs to any great extent, although his advice was sought by thousands and his influence manifest in significant improvements in churches and schools all over the world. His task was the integration of what different types of thinkers and workers were doing. He had the extraordinary ability in evaluating the processes and results of their work. Then by voice and pen he made the best knowledge available to the people who needed guidance.[11]

Cope was in many ways the genius who kept the religious education movement excited and focused.

Throughout his writings one sees reflected a great optimism in what the church could actually achieve in religious education. He was convinced that the church was primarily responsible for the religious training of the young, but he felt that its methods needed to move from those of evangelism and catechism to the "scientific discipline" of education. In fact, Cope reflected a conviction that religious education was more a sub-discipline of education than of theology or ministry. He was much more sophisticated in his understanding of education than he was of theology, particularly ecclesiology. A statement written in one of his first books represents a central conviction which he held throughout his life.

When home and school and lyceum all taught religion the Sunday school may have felt that it could afford to spend its time playing at teaching, in giving a few individuals a chance to take the lesson text and from it to preach so many secondhand sermons to so many little sufferers on successive Sundays. But with the realization of its responsibility for the work of religious education there has come an awakening and a determination to be competent for the task.[12]

Cope's plea was for the church to become competent to the task of religious education.

George Albert Coe, on the other hand, was a creative and original thinker. His influence came from the acuity of his ideas. Like Cope, Coe did not see himself as a theologian, although he more often used theology in his work.[13] He was rather a psychologist of

131

religion studying how persons come to religious faith and how it influenced their action in the world. Coe was clearly in the practical and experiential theological tradition of a William James, concerned with how the faith actually manifested itself in life. Convinced of the importance of scientific research, he wanted to extend it to improve the functioning of the church in society. In one of his intellectual autobiographies, Coe commented that the most significant turning point in his religious development was an ". . . early turning away from dogmatic method to scientific method."[14] Therefore, his work was a scientific pursuit of how religion formed in human personality, and how once formed, it pragmatically affected a person's action in the world and the character of society. For Coe, the end of all education was ethics--decision making in light of the kingdom of God--and the purpose for studying education was to understand how religion could be more effectively organized to shape the world. He declared that the task of the religious educator was ". . . that of re-building the foundations of our society, including the re-creation of religion itself."[15] Religion needed re-formation because no present religion seemed in his view to have the "form and policies" to save society. His social agenda for religious education recovered the missionary impetus of the original Sunday schools.

Some religious educators followed the direction that Coe had set for the future, but more substituted a kind of middle-class character study for his radical social prophecy.[16] His ideas were relativized in a way like those of Dewey. Coe himself was not a practitioner and did not provide the tools for effecting his social agenda; therefore, his ideas were prone to misconception when translated to practice. Personally however he contributed to many "radical" causes, including women's rights, and challenged racism and capitalism. Coe's social program was really never embodied.

Coe was an academician's academician.[17] Here again he can be contrasted to many in his own generation of religious educators. He came to the discipline through thought about religious life rather than experience with the Sunday school. After completing a Ph.D. at Boston University, Coe taught for one year at the University of Southern California and studied in Germany for one more year before joining the faculty of Northwestern University where he officially taught philosophy and pioneered in the discipline of psychology of religion.

His discovery of the scientific method in the study of religion and particularly his work on conversion and the spiritual life convinced him of the truth of developmental psychology. It was this fascination with the developing human personality which sent Coe into the study of religious education. In one of his early books Coe commented that his task was to make public a modern Christianity. He wanted to express how Christian life could be more in tune with modern thought forms represented in scientific method, evolution, the theology of God's immanence, an "exemplar" Christology, and a social interpretation of Jesus' teachings. For him, in modern Christianity salvation occurred by education, rather than blind doctrinal acceptance or emotionalism. By salvation, Coe meant the progressive transformation of the human personality to the divine will expressed in the social-ethical teachings of Jesus.

Coe focused on education because he felt that "the campaign for bringing the world to Christ" would be lost if the church was not improved with modern knowledge and modern methods of religious nurture.[18] In his address to the organizing convention of the REA, he expressed a principle, which was to characterize his life work, that persons could trust contemporary knowledge because God is present in the search for understanding. The church and the world are therefore not in essence separate, but one.

> Accordingly, religious education is not a part of general education, it is general education. It is the whole of which our so-called secular education is only a part or phrase. Religious education alone takes account of the whole personality, of all its powers, all its duties, all its possibilities, and of the ultimate reality of the environment.[19]

For him religious education was the inner meaning of all education.

Throughout his life Coe struggled to relate religious education to understandings about religious personality and to transform all education to an appreciation of its deeply religious and ethical character. Therefore, when Coe was offered a chance in 1909 to teach religious education full-time, he moved to Union Theological Seminary in New York. During these years, Coe continued his involvement with the REA, serving for one term as its president, and there he wrote his most important books on religious education. Five years prior to his retirement Coe was to make one more career move to Teacher's College in New York; yet, he did not leave his commitment to religious education.. After retirement in 1927, Coe continued to write, lecture, involve himself in social causes, and shape the field of religious education until his death in 1952.[20]

Revered by many as the true father of the religious education movement, it is not surprising that Samuel P. Franklin, who was president of the REA the year Coe died, would write, "George Albert Coe was the outstanding religious educator of the first half of the twentieth century. . . . He met the problems of his days in such a spirit and with such resources that the patterns of thought which he molded are still being used in a vital manner and bid fare to be used for years to come."[21] Indeed these comments are still judged to be true. Contemporary church educators still must respond to the foundation Coe set.

In Coe and Cope the spirit of progressive religious education is exhibited. Both reflected the vitality of the movement which still shapes Protestant education. Their agreement on the need for reform, the importance of general education for religious education, the role of the church in the religious education of the public, and the scope of religious education revealed the central convictions of their age.

Assessing the Progressive Church School

Both Cope and Coe were reformers convinced of the importance of religious education and of the crucial role of the church in the culture. Their differences were more subtle than stark. In terms of aim, Cope sought to improve and perfect the "nursery of the church." He sought to make it into the efficient church school. Coe too was concerned with its efficiency and quality, but he focused more on how religious education transformed Christian faith itself. In terms of form, both looked to education and the school to define the proper methods of education. But in terms of scope both looked beyond a school strategy to how education actually occurred in community and culture. Cope focused on the church as learning community while Coe, also interested in the church as community, looked beyond the church to understand religious education in

134

the wider culture. The agreements and differences of
these two significant progressive church educators are
most clearly revealed in their assessment of progress
in church education.

As General Secretary of REA, Cope saw it as his
responsibility to communicate widely the transformations
and progress of the church's school. He was convinced
that the Sunday school in the late nineteenth century
had increasingly become inferior to the public school
and that it would take a great effort to overcome the
image of inferiority. The REA in his analysis had been
the crucial vehicle for transforming the Sunday school
into the church school; therefore, he dated progress in
church education from the founding of REA in 1903. His
general assessment of the growth of church education
is seen in the following summary analysis from his
history of the Sunday school movement.

> No longer neglected by the church, no longer de-
> rided by the schools, no longer the object of
> cheap criticism in the press, no longer calmly
> and uniformly degraded to the basement of the
> church, no longer compelled to carry on a large
> work without financial support from the church,
> but recognized as the great opportunity of the
> church for childhood, as the central and specific
> organization of the church for religious educa-
> tion, supported by public opinion, stimulated by
> great organizations, studied and ordered by ex-
> perts and specialists, facing the future with
> faith and openmindedness; who can tell what the
> coming days may mean to the Sunday school?[22]

The church school he thought had a glorious potential
future since it was now as classified, graded, and
organized as the public school. Frankly, his assessment
was much too optimistic. Church education had neither
solved its image problems, nor upgraded adequately its
program. Nevertheless, his analysis reflects the agenda
or vision which Cope communicated to religious educators.
He wanted to create the church school as a modern educational institution.

In his two ten-year reports on the state of religious education published in 1913 and 1923 respectively,
Cope focused on how church education had moved from
instruction to education.[23] By this distinction he
meant that previous Sunday school "education" had primarily been dogmatic and concerned with the transmission

of content, regardless of its appropriateness to the
pupil or the pupil's readiness; while the new church
school exemplified true education, having subjected itself to scientific research and being concerned with
infusing religion into the processes of individual and
social development.

Cope listed the transformations which had made the
weak Sunday school into a potentially efficient church
school:

1. denominational agencies for religious education
2. seminary and college departments in religious
   education
3. cooperation with public schools in week-day
   schools of religion
4. modern church school buildings
5. graded school organization and curricula
6. professional religious educators
7. interdenominational professional and research
   organizations.[24]

In each of these he reflects his excitement over the
application of scientific pedagogical methods to religious education. In fact, he saw the development of
education and religious education as parallel.

Moreover, Cope praised the church for more clearly
and adequately accepting its educational responsibility.[25] He recognized that the Sunday school had
moved from being a missionary movement outside the
church to becoming a missionary movement for the church.
But he felt that while the church had accepted its mission function, it had never fully accepted its educational function until pushed to do so by twentieth-
century reformers. With the acceptance of the name
"the school of the church" came the conviction that the
local church had to coordinate all of the educational
settings in the life of the church to have a valid educational program.[26] The church school idea then transcended the narrow Sunday school view of church education. Learning and ministry coincided in this educational understanding.

The first two decades of the twentieth century
were therefore understood by Cope as decades of great
potential and progress. He argued three efforts of
human endeavor had converged "into a splendid highway"
which set the future of religious education. The new

sciences of religion, education, and society had merged

> . . . toward the place where both religion and education have taken religious education with increasing seriousness and tend to include it in those great affairs of human life which have a scientific basis, and also, toward the recognition of religious education as a social necessity, as the hope of social salvation.[27]

Cope was indeed optimistic about the progress.

Coe too was caught up in the exuberance of the period with its energy for the transformation of religious education. He too was hopeful; yet while pleased about the progress, he attended more carefully to the issues which were unresolved. For Coe, the progress and reform which had been achieved could most easily be characterized as progress in understanding the science of human personality and its social context and, furthermore, the discovering of methods to affect the personality with religion.[28] This recognition Coe thought was central to the application of scientific pedagogical methods to religious education.

Coe felt that the REA was the crucial agent in the reform of the Sunday school.[29] Its leaders were correct in recognizing that a church educational emergency existed at the turn of the century because Sunday school leaders were increasingly being separated from their public school counterparts. The success of their efforts to integrate more adequately religious education and education he saw as a major victory.[30] Yet, unlike many of his contemporaries, he recognized that some "old-time" Sunday school leaders prior to REA had moved to lay the groundwork for the acceptance of the Sunday school as a real teaching and educational institution.[31] When their concern was coupled with the practice of grading, the surge for progress in church education was made possible.

In defining the progress which had taken place for church education Coe listed:

1. advanced educational methods
2. graded church school organization and graded curricula
3. research in religious education led by college and seminary faculty and the REA

4. critical knowledge of the Bible
5. week-day religious education
6. professional leadership.[32]

As is apparent, both Coe's and Cope's assessments of
the progress in religious education were quite similar.
Their estimations of progress were in fact shared by
many other progressive religious educators.

Nevertheless, while Coe praised the progress which
had been made in transforming the Sunday school to the
educational ideal of scientific psychology and pedagogy, he was concerned that this progress was neither
fast enough, nor sufficient. The inertia of most
churches concerned him. He believed that most had
accepted the new church school ideal, but correspondingly found it difficult to throw off the "theological and educational mindset" which interfered
with the movement to true education. He commented
that, "An unsifted tradition is the main control."[33]
A satisfactory level of pastoral knowledge about education and comprehensive denominational strategies for
education had not yet been reached. He was hopeful
because of the acceptance of the ideas, but he thought
the reality was far from an actuality. Instruction
had to be transformed into education.

Coe did not yet see a satisfactory resolution of
the relation of education and religion. He felt that
neither fully understood their task of affecting the
moral, intellectual, and spiritual climate of the
American people. They were too often seen as parallel
systems. For him general education without a religious
vision and church education without a social vision
were inadequate. In terms of the church, he said,
". . . uncertainty and unsteadiness as to the main
functions of churches in modern society are growing."[34]
Therefore, the primary unfulfilled task of religious
education was to affect the social and spiritual climate of the world. To achieve this end he argued that
Christian religious education must challenge the
Christian religion and the church itself. The task
before Christian education was to remake the Christian
religion that was taught. He argued that, "The main
use and meaning of any vital and growing religion lie
at the precarious edge of life and of civilization.
Consequently the central issue in the education of the
young concerns the unsolved problems of life and of
society."[35] It was therefore not enough for the church
school to be the nursery of the church; it had to be

transformer of the church in light of the kingdom of
God--God's very practical vision for and care for human
life, society, and relationships.

The young were presently being formed more by the
secular culture than by the church and its "walled-in"
religious education. Unless the church took its responsibility of religious and social reconstruction seriously he feared that the message of kingdom would not
be heard, and social exploitation and disintegration
would continue.

Cope and Coe therefore shared many of the same
assessments of the progress of Protestant education,
but they differed on the seriousness with which they
defined the future agenda. They were the contrast of
popularizer and prophet. The social purpose, the
church school form, as well as the widened scope were
shared, but the radicalness of the influence expected
from each was different. Their definitions of purpose,
form, and scope further illustrate the contrasts in
progressive church education.

Purpose

The development of Christian character was the aim
of the church's school for both Cope and Coe. Cope
stated it succinctly in his last published article.
"The story of progress in religious education is that
of movement, under loyalty to the scientific method, to
the vision of a just and happy human society, to a
social program and a social passion that embraces all
mankind."[36] Likewise Coe expressed a similar educational reconstructionism in his classic definition of
Christian education. "It is the systematic, critical
examination and reconstruction of relations between
persons, guided by Jesus' assumption that persons are
of infinite worth, and by the hypothesis of the existence of God, the Great Valuer of Persons."[37] Their
positions are quite similar. The only difference is
with the radicalness with which Coe held his position.
He was willing to move to challenge the church itself,
and he personally moved beyond reflection on Christian
education for social change to write and work for
social change.

Cope argued that the church had the unique responsibility in the American educational system of providing
moral and religious education. In his understanding

139

American democracy itself depended on the church school. Both secular and church school needed to work together to see that society had members who were concerned about social welfare and capable of being participants in social processes. At its core he saw democracy as a religious concept based on the faith that a person could be taught to contribute to society. Its goals were the salvation of society, the sharing by persons of a spiritual ideal and the training of persons for the highest social ends.[38] Therefore, church education had the critical task of educating persons into the highest ideal of character, which he defined as Christian character.

Cope was convinced that this character aim for church education was fundamentally new. Modern church educators, he felt, transcended the instructional and schooling agendas for religious education.[39] Frankly, he seemed unaware that character was a previous aim of Protestant education. Like several unrecognized predecessors, he argued that instruction in knowledge was not sufficient, that the education of the emotions and the development of productive social activity were also required for true education. In fact, he proposed that the test for adequacy in religious education be whether the church really developed Christian character and contributed to the building of a society of good will.[40]

The primary function of religion and consequently religious education which contributed to social life was summarized by Cope in the following manner:

> . . . to so interpret life that men see the good and the true, that they discover and acquire adequate motives, that their desires are stimulated so that they count dear nothing beside . . . the splendid idea of social good, of the love of men, and their life in an ideal family of the divine.[41]

The task of religious education was therefore clearly religious--to inspire culture with a soul. It also was a task best suited to the church because the church was the only social institution concerned with the development of persons to fullness of life, the growth of persons in spiritual life, and the stimulation of society to God's will.[42] Cope sought to influence that church to accept its most significant responsibility of education for faith and democracy.

Coe expressed many of these same goals for the church's school. He was also convinced that the church was the only agency which could effectively carry religious education, but he felt that the bifurcation of education into a two-fold character, secular and religious, was unfortunate.[43] It represented for him an old definition of relationships which was no longer effective in a new cultural time.

Crisis and change were the characteristics which Coe defined as the social context to which religious education needed to respond. He was particularly sensitive to the cultural and intellectual changes which were occurring during the last of the nineteenth century and into the early twentieth century. These changes were seen as causing a crisis of faith and a crisis of social organization. The proliferation of new knowledge, the new corporate style for society, and the increasing social pluralism, as well as the nationalism and social disintegration which resulted from the First World War, had created a new social situation. Both culture and the church, Coe argued, had a monumental task to respond to these changes, even to maintain, much less improve social life.[44]

For Coe the church and religious education were crucial in responding to the new social conditions, for he noted a "sinister drift" in public education to follow the disintegrating drift of society, rather than truly challenging it.[45] The church therefore had to reclaim its prophetic heritage. It had to escape the limited area in which it had been restricted and reclaim the tasks of religious vision, ethical education and social reconstruction. Therefore, while the primary task of religious education was described as that of producing Christian character, Coe called for a ". . . live, vigorous, earth-claiming religion . . . accepting the challenge of our secular civilization by undertaking to convert our industrial and political order into a thing of spiritual significance."[46]

Coe, like Cope, and many other progressive educators saw democracy as an important agenda and ally of religious education, but he was not as trapped in the contemporary American expression of democracy as were many of his colleagues. For Coe the democracy which he sought was the democracy of God (his name for the kingdom of God); therefore, a critical principle was maintained in his relationship with and advocacy of

141

democracy.[47] If it did not promote God's love and
justice and did not emulate the kingdom, he felt it was
false democracy.

He therefore continually asked the embarrassing
question of the effect of religious education. If it
was not expanding the church into the world, and inspiring persons to seek social justice and to work for
the reconstruction of society, he felt that it was
failing.[48] He feared that too often the church became
captive of the culture and lost its power to speak a
word of truth and transformation. Therefore, Coe
challenged the church to re-make itself, to re-make its
version of religion which privatized and separated the
Christian faith from the world, and to re-make society.

> The churches have made a futile and mischievous
> distinction between religious and secular educa-
> tion. . . . Effective religious education must
> be a critique of the culture of our people, and
> an analysis of the forces that are making our
> civilization what it is, and not something
> better.[49]

Coe wanted to see a vital and effective religious education which could shape life and character in light
of God's transforming and loving presence.

The distinction between Cope and Coe can be
described as that of a religious transmitter and a
religious transformer. More accurately it is the distinction between a person who trusted the church to be
and represent the eternal church; and one who challenged
the church to be more faithful.[50] Cope worked within
the structures of the church to perfect its educational
system and effect. Coe however sought to transform
the church itself into a more faithful representation
of God's kingdom. Christian character was an agenda
for both, but its definition and how it was to be formed
were different. The distinction is much like that between Dewey and some of his followers; whereas Dewey
sought to reconstruct social life, his followers per-
sonalized and privatized social relations. Coe sought
a faithful church, while Cope sought to make it more
efficient.

142

Form and Scope

Both Cope and Coe looked to educational theory and school practice to inform and to enhance the church's educational ministry. Neither, though, was narrowly restricted to the church school. Both saw it as only one agency of education. More informed by the discipline of pedagogy itself, they argued that a community approach to church education was best and sought to understand the unique educative agencies of the church and to coordinate them into a total program. Therefore, in their views form and scope cannot be separated. Religious education was a program which coordinated the church into a community/school of Christian living.

In particular, it was the focus on the child as the subject of education and the processes of graded instruction which had been most significant for them. Such a focus transformed education from being the transmission of dogmatic content to being an interactive process matching religious content and experience with the experience, needs, and natural processes of development of the learner.[51] Coe pointed particularly to Horace Bushnell as a Christian forebearer of such a stance in religious education; for, he saw Bushnell as a challenger of the doctrine of depravity, and as a respecter of the child as child.[52] To reform the church's education, they advocated principles of psychological growth and development. Cope encouraged the publication of articles on child development and he himself described a graded pattern for church education, and Coe edited a graded Sunday school curriculum.[53]

Of the two, Cope however attempted more directly to describe how a modern church education program could be developed. Coe centered most of his energies in developing the theory of religious education, usually just giving hints of the practical forms for his ideas.[54] In contrast, Cope described in detail methods which were needed to be progressive.[55] The descriptions of neither Cope nor Coe differ significantly and they are in tune with general progressive church theory and practice.

Both emphasized the notion of coordination within the educational life of the church. Their concern for the notions of development had pushed both of them beyond schooling. They affirmed that development

143

occurred throughout the whole of life and therefore
good education took seriously the various life settings where persons learned. The school was only one
example of pedagogy. In fact, Coe argued at one point
that some school leaders themselves were not even being
faithful to the content of scientific education.[56]
Consequently, both advocated a coordinated, comprehensive church program which respected the religious and
educational character of the church itself.

Cope described such a comprehensive program in
Religious Education in the Church. He argued that the
church, as a social institution for spiritual growth,
was itself an educational agency. It did not need to
be transformed in an "academic hall" with teachers
wearing "college gowns" to be educational.[57] Its very
nature was to be educational. Therefore church leaders
needed to recognize the church as a religious society
and develop an intentional, clearly defined program.
Such a program would coordinate worship, preaching,
evangelism, social life, social service, youth activities, family life, and formal schooling.[58] To achieve
such a coordination Cope advocated trained religious
education leadership, new church educational buildings,
and expanded church support and funding.[59] Cope thought
that such a coordinated program built on the best of
the school concurred with educational theory and would
transform the church into an effective educational
agency.

Coe agreed with most of these views, in fact his
writings were probably their primary source. As early
as 1904 he had described how the church school was more
than the formal Sunday school religion. It was ". . .
the organization of the church and the family into educational unity."[60] He described how trained leadership
and a coordinated program could build the church as
school.

In A Social Theory of Religious Education Coe refined these ideas. He argued that religion histori-
cally embodied itself into "tribes, nations, churches,
and parties" which were themselves the context for
education. He went farther to argue that ". . . a
church makes its members more than the members make the
church."[61] In describing how church life, worship, the
family, and the school could work together and be
related to a person's experience in the world, Coe
developed a comprehensive conception of the church as

144

educator. Within this conception, he also argued that
the church was the coordinator of the larger community's
program of religious education.

Coe went beyond the mere description of how church
agencies could be coordinated to describe the principles on which this coordination was based. Since the
church was an intentional community seeking the democracy of God, he argued that it had a goal which protected it from intellectualism or privatism, and which
maintained its radical ethical and prophetic character.[62] Coe translated his radical agenda of the reconstruction of religion and society into his suggestions for practice. In this way he built on ideas such
as Cope's but he focused them in a clearer theological
and ethical direction. He attempted to maintain a
prophetic practice to fulfill his prophetic agenda.

Coe feared a practice like Cope's for he felt that
it could fall into the danger of teaching a method
which failed to be faithful because the church which it
coordinated was itself unfaithful. Coe had too often
experienced the church as falling into traditionalism,
institutionalism, and denominational introversion.[63]
Since such a church would tend uncritically to perpetuate its traditionalism, institutionalism, and
introversion, that church needed a reborn Christian
education that would challenge it to social radicalism.

> We need a fellowship of repentence, of radical
> self-commitment, of faith and hope that dare the
> utmost. But this means that the church is to be
> distinguished by the extremeness of its social
> radicalism. It is to be the mother of radicalisms,
> and the companion and support of all who, in any
> sphere of life, take persons as the true wealth
> of the world.[64]

The primary question for Coe was not how were the educational agencies of the church coordinated, but how
did the church become a self-critical people who were
in search of the kingdom and who created a radical
reaching community of love and faithfulness.

Of course, Cope too would have hoped for a church
which educated in such a manner as to build Christian
character and transform social life, but as too many
other educators his concern with method did overshadow
his definition of goals and aims in such a manner that
he did not directly ask how these practices fulfilled

his goals. Much the same was the case for both progressive church education and progressive education. The concern for method blunted the realization of the radical goals of personal and social reconstruction. Liberal religious education can be criticized for a lack of effectiveness because many of its proponents failed to transcend the present state of the church in their practice. Too often the inertia in the church itself, which Coe recognized, was ignored. Coe argued that education which perpetuated the inertia, no matter what its theory, form, or scope would not result in transformation. In contrast with many other progressives, Coe sought to integrate the theological rationale and practical effort.

Sunday School and Church School

In Henry Frederick Cope and George Albert Coe, the best of the progressive tradition in religious education found voice. The agenda of this tradition was Christian character, yet its radicalness was defined variously; its form was drawn from educational theory, but the relationship of public and religious education was left unanswered; and its scope sought to include the total life of the church, but its definitions of church varied. It was also a tradition which usually focused on the internal life of the church and the developing needs of persons, rather than the reconstruction of society. Finally, it was a tradition which often ignored its roots, yet in all was not much different from its roots.

Like its predecessor, the Sunday school, progressive religious education defined the church school as the nursery of the church, its goal was Christian character, its form was drawn from that of the school, and its scope was coextensive with the life of the church. Its lack of clarity about the relation of church to culture, and the real impact of Christian education on the Christian community and the world also is continuous with the past of the Sunday school.

In persons like Cope, one sees heroic attempts to improve the church's educational ministry; yet one is reminded by persons like Coe of the gaps in these efforts. He reminds us that when the church baptized the Sunday school, it did so without resolving the theological and practical issues of integrating the Sunday school and church community, and of integrating

146

church education with the education of the public. The
task for church education is to address these issues as
well as define the educational role of the church in
the wider culture. Coe argued that every human social
problem required ". . . the common human need for in-
spiration, for the divine in breathing of hope, for un-
compromising love, for far-sight, for letting go the
half-gods in a great and ultimate faith in Fatherhood
and Brotherhood."[65] Such a comprehensive vision of the
significance and mission of the church may provide a
way of beginning to address the relation of church
education to the education of the public. A recognition of the continuities and unanswered questions is
therefore a place to begin.

Notes

[1]George A. Coe, "Mr. Cope's Unique Contribution to Our
Generation," Religious Education 18 (October 1923):264.

[2]Hugh Hartshorne, "George Albert Coe," Religious Education
22 (January 1927):100.

[3]Henry F. Cope, Organizing the Church School: A Comprehensive Scheme for Religious Educational Activities for Children
and Youth (Garden City, NY: Doubleday, Doran and Co., 1929),
pp. 30-32.

[4]See the following articles by George A. Coe: "Discussion
of the Bower, Cole and Smith Papers," Religious Education 31
(April 1936):116; "The Elusiveness of 'Religion'," Religious Education 31 (January 1936):43-45; and "Our Two-Headed System of
Education: The Problem Defined," Religious Education 22 (June
1927):564-565.

[5]Adelaide Teague Case, "Christian Education," in The Church
Through Half a Century, ed. Samuel McCrea Cavert and Henry Pitney
Van Dusen (New York: Charles Scribner's Sons, 1936), pp. 229-
247. For background see also her Liberal Christianity and Reli-
gious Education: A Study of Objectives in Religious Education
(New York: MacMillan Co., 1924).

[6]See for example two articles by William Clayton Bower, "Points of Tension between Progressive Religious Education and Current Theological Trends," Religious Education 34 (July-September 1939):164-172; and "Points of Tension between Modern Religious Education and Current Theological and Social Trends," Religious Education 35 (April-June 1939):69-73. Also the controversy is still apparent in a statement and responses written for the REA by Chave, Coe, Bower and other progressive educators in 1950 in "Religious Education for Liberal Progressives: A Statement and Evaluations," Religious Education 45 (March-April 1950):67-100.

[7]Most of the following historical survey of the life of Henry Cope is drawn from Theodore G. Soares, "Henry Frederick Cope, His Life and Work," Religious Education 18 (October 1923): 317-324; and Idem et al., "In Memoriam: Henry Frederick Cope," Religious Education 18 (October 1923):260-307.

[8]Coe, "Mr. Cope's Unique Contribution to Our Generation," p. 264; and Soares, "Henry Frederick Cope, His Life and Work," p. 322.

[9]"Teacher Training Commission of the Religious Education Association: Report of Committee on Elementary and Advanced Teacher-Training Courses for Sunday Schools," by Walter S. Athearn, Chm., Religious Education 7 (April 1912):83.

[10]Henry F. Cope, The Evolution of the Sunday School (Boston: Pilgrim Press, 1911); Idem, "Ten Years' Progress in Religious Education," Religious Education 13 (June 1913):117-149; and Idem, "Twenty Years' Progress in Religious Education," Religious Education 18 (October 1923):307-316.

[11]Soares, "Henry Frederick Cope, His Life and Work," p. 320.

[12]Henry F. Cope, The Modern Sunday School in Principle and Practice, 2nd ed. (New York: Fleming H. Revell Co., 1907), p. 10.

[13]Coe's most theological book is his What is Christian Education? (New York: Charles Scribner's Sons, 1929) where he discusses the nature of the kingdom of God as motivating vision for religious education. His importance as a psychologist of religion can be seen in his early book on conversion, The Spiritual Life: Studies in the Science of Religion (New York: Eaton and Mains, 1900) and his later The Psychology of Religion (Chicago: University of Chicago Press, 1916).

[14]George A. Coe, "My Search for What Is Most Worthwhile," Religious Education 47 (March-April 1952):176.

[15]"Dr. Coe's Remarks," Religious Education 22 (April 1927): 436. See also Coe, "My Search for What is Most Worthwhile," pp. 173-174.

[16]One representative of this trend is George Herbert Betts, The Character Outcome of Present-Day Religion (New York: Abingdon Press, 1931). Many others moved away from theology, social criticism, and the church all together muting the power of God's plea as expressed by Coe. Like Dewey, Coe had his simplistic followers.

[17]Most of the following biographical comments are drawn from articles published in Religious Education at Coe's retirement from Teacher's College in 1927 and his death in 1952. See particularly Hartshorne, "George Albert Coe," and a series in Religious Education 47 (March-April 1952):67-96 where William Clayton Bower, Ernest J. Chave, Harry F. Ward, Charles S. Braden, Arthur L. Swift, Jr., and Margaret Forsythe discuss his life and contribution. Also a dissertation has been completed on Coe, Helen Archibald, "George Albert Coe: Theorist for Religious Education in the Twentieth Century" (Ph.D. dissertation, University of Illinois at Urbana-Champaign, 1975).

[18]George Albert Coe, The Religion of a Mature Mind (Chicago: Fleming H. Revell Co., 1902), pp. 8, 294-295.

[19]George Albert Coe, "Religious Education as a Part of General Education," in Who Are We? The Quest for a Religious Education, ed. John Westerhoff III (Birmingham: Religious Education Press, 1978), p. 20.

[20]In this study primary reference will be made to the works which Coe wrote prior to his retirement. This decision reflects the focus of this part of the study on understanding the heyday of the progressive church education movement which began to wane with the depression. Coe's later works were still of significance. The only difference they reflect is a growing frustration with the difficulty to reform church education and with its seeming ineffectiveness in enabling ethical and political decision making.

[21]Samuel P. Franklin, "The Religious Education Association Approaches Its Fiftieth Year," Religious Education 47 (March-April 1952):66.

[22]Cope, Evolution of the Sunday School, pp. 152-153.

[23]Cope, "Ten Years' Progress, p. 118; and Idem, "Twenty Years' Progress," pp. 307, 312-314.

[24]Cope, "Twenty Years Progress," p. 307; and Idem, "Ten Years' Progress, pp. 120-125.

[25]Cope, "Twenty Years' Progress," pp. 312-313; Idem, Evolution of Sunday School, pp. 108-114; and Idem, "Ten Years' Progress," pp. 125-126.

[26]Cope, Evolution of Sunday School, p. 124; and Idem, "Ten Years' Progress, p. 126.

[27]Cope, "Twenty Years' Progress," p. 314.

[28]Coe, "My Search for What is Most Worthwhile," p. 170; and Idem, "Burning Issues," Religious Education 23 (Special Convention Issue 1928):649-650.

[29]Coe, "Burning Issues," p. 649; and Idem, "Annual Survey of Progress in Religious and Moral Education," Religious Education 4 (April 1909):7.

[30]Coe, "Burning Issues," p. 649. See also George Albert Coe, Education in Religion and Morals (Chicago: Fleming H. Revell Co., 1904), p. 6; and Idem, "The President's Annual Address: New Reasons for Old Duties," Religious Education 5 (April 1910):4-5.

[31]Coe, Education in Religion and Morals, p. 287.

[32]See Coe, "Burning Issues," pp. 649-652; and Idem, Education in Religion and Morals, pp. 286-301.

[33]Coe, What Is Christian Education? p. 14.

[34]Ibid., p. 15. See also Idem, "Burning Issues," p. 651; Dr. Coe's Remarks," p. 436; and Idem, "Let Us Rethink the Purpose of Religious Education," Religious Education 23 (December 1928): 974-975.

[35]Coe, "Burning Issues," p. 652.

[36]Cope, "Twenty Years' Progress," p. 314.

[37]Coe, What Is Christian Education? p. 296.

[38]Henry F. Cope, Education for Democracy (New York: Mac-millan Co., 1920), pp. 28-33, 42-51.

[39]Henry F. Cope, Religious Education in the Church (New York: Charles Scribner's Sons, 1918), pp. 28-35. See also Idem, Modern Sunday School, p. 61.

[40]Cope, Evolution of Sunday School, p. 124; and Idem, Religious Education in Church, pp. 23-26.

[41]Cope, Education for Democracy, p. 35.

[42]Cope, Religious Education in Church, p. 40.

[43]Coe, "President's Annual Address," p. 4; and Idem, A Social Theory of Religious Education (New York: Charles Scribner's Sons, 1917), pp. 260-262.

[44]These notions progressively grow throughout Coe's writings. See the following writings which are listed chronologically: Religion of a Mature Mind, pp. 5-10; Education in Religion and Morals, p. 6; "Annual Survey of Progress in Religious and Moral Education," pp. 8-15; "Our Two-Headed System," pp. 564-567; "The Religious Outlook of the World Today," Religious Education 31 (April 1936):85-90; and "The Assault Upon Liberalism," Religious Education 34 (April-June 1939):85-92.

[45]Coe, "Our Two-Headed System," pp. 565-566. It is interesting that Coe quotes Cubberley to support his position. See also George A. Coe, "Religious Education and Political Conscience," Teachers College Record 23 (September 1922):297-304.

[46]Coe, "Burning Issues," p. 652.

[47]This theme is most clearly developed in Coe's classic book A Social Theory of Religious Education. See particularly pages vii-x, 53-63, 248-265.

[48]Examples from both his early and later writing are: "Annual Survey of Progress in Religious and Moral Education," p. 7; "Burning Issues," p. 651; and "Religious Outlook," p. 89.

[49]Coe, "Let Us Rethink the Purpose of Religious Education,"
p. 978.

[50]Note that this distinction is similar to that between
Vincent and Eggleston in Chapter III. While Vincent worked within the church to improve its education, Eggleston challenged it
to reach out and be more faithful to its mission responsibility.

[51]Coe, "Religious Education as a Part of General Education,"
p. 15; and Idem, Education in Religion and Morals, pp. 98-118;
Cope, Modern Sunday School, pp. 62-72; and Idem, Evolution of
Sunday School, pp. 111-125.

[52]Coe, Religion of Mature Mind, pp. 305-315.

[53]Henry F. Cope, Modern Sunday School and Its Present Day
Task (New York: Fleming H. Revell Co., 1907-1916), pp. 200-214;
and George A. Coe, The Core of Good Teaching, A Sunday-School
Curriculum, Completely Graded Series (New York: Charles
Scribner's Sons, 1911).

[54]Outlines of church education programs are included in the
following books of Coe: Core of Good Teaching, pp. 7-18; Education in Religion and Morals, pp. 271-323; and Social Theory, pp.
226-247.

[55]The following three books are explicit descriptions of the
practice of the church school: Modern Sunday School; Religious
Education in Church; and Organizing the Church School.

[56]"Our Two-Headed System," p. 566.

[57]Cope, Religious Education in Church, p. 39.

[58]Ibid. A section is devoted to each of these themes in the
book. See also Idem, Organizing the Church School, pp. 128-129.

[59]Ibid., p. 245.

[60]Coe, Education in Religion and Morals, pp. 288-289.

[61]Coe, Social Theory, p. 85.

[62]Ibid., p. 341.

[63]Coe, What Is Christian Education? p. 240.

[64]Ibid., p. 254. See also Social Theory, pp. 341-342.

[65]Coe, Social Theory, p. 265.

CHAPTER VII

FROM NURSERY OF THE CHURCH

TO EDUCATION OF THE PUBLIC

For the twenty-fifth anniversary of the founding of the Religious Education Association (REA) in 1928, George Herbert Betts, then Professor of Christian Education at Northwestern University, was asked to summarize the future tasks of Protestant church education. He focused in his remarks on "perennial tasks" of religious education. By this description he hoped to communicate that educational practices are in continual need of improvement, yet he did more.[1] What he really communicated was a definition of the condition of Protestant education. His definition along with his listing of issues parallels that of other church educators for the previous seventy-five years.

Fundamental to Betts' understanding was the conviction that the church had finally awakened to the importance of education in the process of Christianization. The Sunday school had been transformed with great effort into the "educational consciousness" of the church concerned with a mode of salvation in which the processes of human development were taken seriously and whose goals were Christian character and conduct. While Betts felt that the transformation was far from complete, he did believe that the REA had achieved much progress in its twenty-five year history.

To continue the progress in religious education, "[t]o awaken this giant [the Protestant Church], help him to get the sleep out of his eyes and his mind cleared for action . . .," Betts listed five tasks:

1. the training of ministers in education
2. the development of true educational standards for church schools
3. the improvement of church school teachers
4. the clarification of the developmental and conduct goals for religious education
5. the relating of home and church in Christian education.[2]

In all of these recommendations, Betts hoped to move the institution of the church school to embody in practice the progressive philosophy. He wanted clear evidence of character change as the goal; adequate educational buildings, curricula, and teachers as the form; and a clear linkage of church, home, and education as the scope.

These "perennial tasks" had in fact been the perennial agenda for Sunday/church school reformers since the middle of the nineteenth century. To highlight the continuity of these tasks from the time the Sunday school became a church agency, all that is needed is to rehearse some of the previous statements of the agenda for the Sunday/church school. For example, at the Fifth National Sunday School Convention in 1872 when the uniform lesson curriculum was approved, a list was made of plans for increasing the interest and efficiency of the Sunday school. The difficulties to be overcome which were listed can be summarized as follows: (a) the lack of full acceptance by the church of its educational responsibility, (b) the lack of an efficient educational organization and staff, and (c) the lack of a significant evidence of change in the pupil.[3]

In the 1890s, William Reynolds, the field superintendent for the International Sunday School Association, again restated tasks of Christian education. He argued that the church had been given a divine call to be a missionary institution and to do so through preaching and teaching; therefore he listed improved educational organization and training, cooperation with public education, Sunday school publications, and increased church responsibility as evidence of progress.[4] The agenda was further focused for the old-time reformers by John Vincent and A. R. Taylor at the turn of the century when they expressed a hopeful assessment of the future of the Sunday school. They thought it could achieve full status as an educational institution and become a full partner in a program of religious education combining church, school, and home.[5]

Finally, the perennial agenda was reflected for the new progressive reformers in the founding of the International Sunday School Council of Religious Education which called for a coordinated, comprehensive, and professional church educational program with adequate time, staff, curriculum, and equipment.[6] Only by fulfilling such an agenda did they feel that the church would begin to complete its educational responsibility.

Indeed while there had been significant change in
the time since the Sunday school had become an agency
of the church, that change was within a structure, a
perennial agenda, and a foundational definition for
church educational practice. Many who felt that they
advocated new directions to overcome past recalcitrant
structures in fact shared the same goals about purpose
and form as had earlier creators of those structures.
Such is the story of the perennial tasks of religious
education.

The Character of the Church School:
Toward a Revisionist Interpretation

Initially the Sunday school was a school for children who would otherwise not have had the opportunity
for education. Its task was to teach on Sunday,
reading, writing, arithmetic, religion, and morality to
children who worked the other six days a week in fac-
tories. Transplanted from England to America, the Sunday school continued to be a missionary and philanthropic endeavor, usually outside the church, to reclaim
the children of the city for Christianity and to extend
the saving word of Christianity into the frontier.

With the emergence of the public school movement
in America, in which many religious leaders were in
volved, the original purpose of the Sunday school became antiquated. A new definition of the task of the
Sunday school was needed. Sunday school leaders and
some church leaders concluded that the Sunday school
and the public school must develop a cooperative relationship. The public school was to teach reading,
writing, and arithmetic. The public school was to form
moral American persons committed to the ideal of the
American democratic republic. The Sunday school, on the
other hand, was to become the educational agency of the
church. While some explicit educational functions of
the original Sunday school were to be transferred to
the public school, the Sunday school was to become the
place where the educational goals of Christianity were
focused.

Selling this idea of the Sunday school as the educational agent of the church and in symbiotic relationship with the public school was not easy. The church
had other options from which to choose to fulfill its
educational goals: confirmation training, catechism,

157

preaching, the Methodist classes and bands, and private
school systems, to name a few. Yet, in most Protestant
denominations, excluding to a great extent Lutherans,
Episcopalians, and, for a time, Presbyterians, the
Sunday school became the primary Protestant educational
agency. It moved from an institution independent of
the church to an independent institution within the
church, and from a religious school teaching secular
subjects to a church school teaching religion. By the
1870s this new notion about Christian education practice was well established.[7] Protestant education was
given what became an enduring identity, form, and
scope.

First, the identity of that institution is described by the phrase "the nursery of the church."[8]
The task of the Sunday school was to teach the children
of the faithful denominational religion and to direct
them into the church. In fact, by 1890 the new field
secretary of the International Sunday School Convention
could claim that eighty-three percent of all new church
members came through the Sunday school.[9] The Sunday
school thus became the primary entry point into the
church. Its tasks were defined as conversion and
edification: To mold the character of its own members
and their children, and to prepare them to do the work
of the church.[10] It is this identity which continues
into the present. Decisions about educational theory
and practice have since had to pass this test of
identity.

Second, the primary form which was developed for
the work of the church's education was that of school.
As early as the 1860s the school was becoming the primary public model for the practice of education. While
there has always been a sense of ambivalence in church
educators about the relation of the public school to
the church school which is characterized by a conviction that the church school's religious goals must
take precedence over the public school's instructional
goals, the school was still chosen as the form for
church education.

From the mid-1800s, a complementary relationship
was built between the Sunday school and the public
school. For the first fifty years, the public school
learned much from the Sunday school in terms of procedures and methods, but by the turn of the century
that relationship had shifted. The public school had

moved much faster in subscribing to a corporate definition of the educational system. Therefore, definitions of effective educational practice came almost
exclusively from the public school. The Sunday school
maintained many of its connections to the factory version of the system of education and thus became known
as a poor representative of the school model.

Educational criticism of the work of the church's
school so concerned some church educators that they
worked to transform the school of the church into an
effective educational agency. Most attempts to upgrade the Sunday school were exclusively concerned with
educational practice, rather than theological content.
Elmer Barnes, for example, exclaimed, we cannot ". . .
permanently employ methods out of harmony with the
methods of secular education."[11] Also Walter Athearn,
a professor at Boston University, went so far as to
suggest that a religious education system be created
fully equivalent to the public school system in time,
teachers, curriculum, and consequences.[12] In such a
way, Athearn hoped to make church education effective
as a force in the forming of the American character.
That the Sunday school must stop "playing at teaching"
was the common agreement.

The form of church education has been heavily influenced by what one could call, a "public school
philosophy of education." This influence was heightened
during the transition from factory to corporate model
of education. Issues of the management of a school,
the structure of the classroom, the training of
teachers, the institutional readiness of pupils, and the
design of the curriculum became even more important.

While these issues were always important for the
church's school, several leaders and critics of the
church's education argued that such exclusive focus on
them obscured more important questions of defining
the relation of education to the church's ministry and
the relation of theology to the praxis of education.
Some critics felt that too often questions of method
and procedure were raised over those of theory.

The question of the scope of the church's education
became an enduring concern. In theory most church education leaders sought to relate the church's school to
the broader ministry of the congregation and to a
broader ecology of public and church institutions.

Relating church, family, and church's school has been the primary definition of scope. Yet how to realize this relationship has also been an enduring concern of church education.

While in theory the Sunday school was the central entry point into the life of the church, in practice an uneasy relationship between education and ministry persisted. The independence of the early Sunday school has too often continued. For example, church educators have concurrently complained that the church did not make adequate provision for its functioning, while they remained aloof from the ministry of the congregation. They have requested that the church recruit new members for the church's school, financially support it, make provision for adequate facilities, support teachers, and encourage the pastor to participate in its program. Yet at the same time, many church schools have continued to hold their own worship services, many classes have functioned as small churches, and the teaching in classes has been often a separate preaching service. The theology of this teaching has also often been at odds with the official denominational position and the words of the pulpit. For example, William Kennedy of Union Theological Seminary has argued that the Sunday school has always had too little religion for the church and too much for the public school.[13]

Separation and simplicity are the key issues which caused the lack of resolution of the question of scope. No matter how much religious education leaders talked about coordinating religious education with the life of the parish and introducing adequate methods of Biblical criticism and theological reflection, a sharp wall existed between the theory of Christian education and its implementation in the school of the church. The relation of the identity of church education, its form, and its scope remain in conflict.

Christian educators often blamed the church and its ministry for the lack of resolution. One example is the position taken at the 1930 meeting of International Council of Religious Education. While the council adopted the motto "Every church a school in Christian living" and decided that the total life of the church was the only proper environment for education, the participants concluded that pastors would not understand this new idea and many church people would resist it. Therefore, until pastors and laity could be educated, they proposed that a proximate objective be attempted, that the church school should be made into ". . . a school of Christian living maintained and administered by the church."[14] The planned success of this proximate objective was to teach pastors the potential of education. Here the separation of the church and Christian education was not only recognized but affirmed as essential for a future unity.

While the identity of church education was defined as the nursery of the church, in practice its relation to the church has been confused. In an attempt to build and improve their own institution, Christian educators have not clearly dealt with the implications of being a ministry of the church. It is this historic conflict within the self-understanding of church education and the uneasy relationship of membership goals, ministry goals, and form that maintain the lack of clarity.

The way the issues of identity, form, and scope have been resolved is the reason why efforts of church educators at reform in church education have often been blocked or redirected. While believing in the contribution of education to the ministry of the church, actions which seem to suggest that Christian education cannot really be integrated with the total life of the church, coupled with the desire to perfect the church school as a separate educational institution, have contradicted that belief. In practice, church educators have acted as if the next educational innovation or the next new curriculum would provide an answer to their dilemma, rather than reassessing the basic "system" of church education. Moreover, the lack of awareness about foundational assumptions along with the natural propensity to maintenance which seems built into institutions has resulted in the crucial problem of inertia which Coe highlighted. Without a clear awareness of what needs to be changed, or whether it does; how the change would affect the "system" of church education; and how church education, church and culture relate in an institutional ecology, efforts at change or reform are difficult.

This problem of inertia has been recognized by some church education scholars, but suggestions beyond that of awareness have not been often offered. For example, in his twenty-fifth anniversary address, Betts reluctantly concluded ". . . the Protestant church, both in its laity and its clerical leadership (taken on the average), is still unawake to the possibilities for the church and the individual which lie in the education of the young in religion."[15] To combat this problem, Betts called for education of the church to its educational tasks and rewards.

Supporting the perception of inertia William Kennedy, in his contemporary history of the formative years of the Sunday school, asserted that the institutional power which the nineteenth century Sunday school gained catapulted its form into the twentieth. He concluded,

> . . . the inertia of such a massive force, institutionalized independently, with its simplistic system of study and thought, contributed to American Christianity's failure to produce as highly sophisticated and relevent a theology as might otherwise have been the case during the past century.[16]

Furthermore, Kennedy concluded that the inertia complicated the search for a definition of the church in America and linked the church to the culture predominantly as maintainer, rather than challenger.[17]

Kennedy's comments are reminders of those of Coe who suggested that the problem for church education was not in the goals adopted as much as in the form which the Christian religion took in American culture.[18] The problem of inertia as understood by Coe could only be addressed if the Christian religion were remade by the process of education itself. The relation of church to culture, the religious education configuration, and the practical vision of the kingdom were primary agendas for Christian educators. The resolution of these issues was for him a prolegomena to the discipline of Christian education.

Building on Coe's analysis and actual evidence of inertia and continuity in the theory and practice of Protestant church education, certain suggestions can be made for directions in educational policy in Protestant churches. Briefly those directions are that Christian educators must fundamentally address the question of the nature of the church and its ministry, for the question of church education cannot be separated from that of the church itself. Moreover, the relation of church to culture and consequently the present ecology of and for Christian religious education cannot be ignored. The church may be the central agent of Christian religious education, but it has to function within a broader configuration of teaching institutions and educational strategies. Finally, the actual desired effect of church education on the church, individual character, and the culture must be addressed. In other words, the goals of church education are theological issues about the character of Christian life. These implications must be explored in relation to the prevailing questions of purpose, form, and scope to describe policy directions for Christian religious education.

Purpose, Form, and Scope: The Religious Education of the Public

While the Sunday school and church school were consistently defined as the nursery of the church where Christian character was to be formed, some church educators wondered whether this was indeed possible. They wondered whether incorporation into the church and the formation of Christian character were compatible.

Coe would argue that incorporation into some forms of the church formed persons who were more committed to maintaining the church itself, rather than really transforming it into the prophetic, world-engaging community of persons which it is called to be. Coe's suspicions were in fact demonstrated in a 1927 REA-sponsored survey of how individual denominations actually conceived of and practiced church education. Through the survey, it was revealed that while for most denominations religious education was conceived ". . . as the chief instrument for building the church of the future and for the progressive realization of the Kingdom of God," that several denominations were actually more concerned with how children or youth accepted their part in the institution of the church or accepted the essential teachings of the denomination.[19] Institutional maintenance or dogmatic acceptance of denominational differences was judged by the REA researchers as in the way of character development.

What is exhibited here is a theological difference. For some ecclesiologies, education in Christian character would mean incorporation into an institution and for others it would mean becoming a servant to the

163

world.[20] Fundamentally, then the question of the purpose of Christian religious education is a theological
question rooted in a definition of the nature of the
church and of the church's relation to the world. Too
often, it seems, church educators have failed to submit
their goals to theological analysis and have rather
relied on educational theory for their goals. Dwayne
Huebner of Yale University Divinity School has suggested
that church educators have tended to be ". . . blinded
to the need to rethink the linkage between religion and
education by rays of worldly hope originating in secular
education."[21] Huebner suggests that religious education
is a discipline both drawn from educational theory and
the study of religion (for Christianity: the study of
Christian religion). The goals, form, and scope for
religious education are to be drawn from both sources.
Huebner encourages religious educators to engage in
interpretive and integrative thinking drawing faithfully from both sources.

Such integrative thinking would mean that church
educators would seek to understand generally how persons
in Christian religion are educated. In addition, they
would seek to understand both the various philosophies
of education and the theologies of Christian life.
Such study could result in an interpretation of some
patterns of how theology and the human science of education can be integrated. Yet even at the end of this
process, decisions have to be made in terms of a faith
orientation and fundamental life loyalty. Such is the
process exhibited best in both Eggleston and Coe. Both
drew on a critical understanding of the character of
Christian life and the nature of the church as well as
the emerging science of education.[22]

One possible direction for the future for Christian
education could be to rethink and extend the work of
Eggleston and Coe. The task is to seek to discover how
a person can be educated into a prophetic community
actually seeking to be faithful to the vision of the
kingdom of God. Such an endeavor would draw from the
life of Christian religion and the social world, but
it would remake both in the process. It would become
a Christian religious education of the public seeking
to make the Christian religion an important voice in
the development of American culture. The crucial questions would address the nature of Christian life and
mission and the relation of the Christian church to the
American culture.

The work of Martin Marty, a church historian, and
Lawrence Cremin, an educational historian, suggest some
means to extend today the notion of education for
prophetic community. Marty presents an interpretation
of the public role of the church while Cremin describes
the context of public education.

Marty argues that amidst the pluralism and "consu-
mer" character of the modern religious scene in which
religious groups compete to sell their religious "products," that a convergence of religious forces has
occurred which can clarify and extend the church's public role. He calls this new phenomenon, the "public
church," because it consists of elements from mainline
Protestantism, Roman Catholicism, and the new evangelicalism who are all committed to ". . . the res pub-
lica, the public order that surrounds and includes
people of faith."23 The public church is essentially a
"communion of communions" because each lives with its
own traditions, while sharing a common commitment to a
public vocation. At its core, the public church seeks
to relate the gospel and the modern world context believing that they inform each other and that a gospel
mandate is to take the Christian message into the world
seeking to humanize the world in light of the kingdom
of God.

In his analysis Marty describes a possible direction for the church in the contemporary world. He is
convinced that all of the resources are available for
the church to claim a public role, but it is necessary
for the public churches to discover this convergence
and their common commitments. "The public church does
not await invention but discovery. When its participants recognize its scope, they can better realize their
possibilities both individually and as a community."24

What the public church provides is an alternative
way of understanding the church in the world. Marty
contrasts the public church with a modern secularism
which would seek to ignore the presence of the transcendent, and correspondingly, of religious groups who
are locked into a tribalism ignoring the world. Both
of these tendencies relegate the church to privatistic
religious expressions dealing with matters of personal
and family identity. They blunt the role the church
can play at the intersection of gospel and modern
world.

Crucial for the discovery and development of the
public church however is new attention to education
and evangelism.[25] In a religious world characterized
by "marketing," the church seems forced to either create
its own tribe walled off from the world where a "cognitive minority" can be maintained, or, in contrast,
take a clearly apologetic stance speaking the word of
the gospel in such a way that it demands cognitive
attention in the public world. To Marty, church education has too often failed at this last agenda; therefore, traditioning and education are crucial. The
strategy for education however must recognize commitment and pluralism, certainty and ambiguity, and private and public. The resources for education are the
traditions, spiritual experiences, symbols, narratives,
and theologies of the churches. But these must be
brought in relation to the new knowledge, social conditions, and community responsibilities of the world
context. Faithfulness demands, to Marty's perspective,
involvement with the world and education that seeks to
link world and Christian faith. It is clear from his
analysis, and that of other historians of American religion, that most education even religious education takes
place through cultural socialization.[26] Church educators need to discover how the church's education can
significantly participate in the wider educational context.

The educational analysis of Cremin may provide a
way for church educators to understand this wider educational ecology. To Cremin, American educators have
wrongly put the burden of education on the public school.
Enthused with professional pride, they have claimed too
much for themselves and their institution. Public education is, to Cremin, clearly not limited to the formal
institution of the school. "The important fact is that
family life does educate, religious life does educate,
and organized work does educate; and, what is more,
the education of all three realms is as intentional as
the education of the school, however different in kind
and quality."[27] Moreover, mass media, voluntary organizations, public libraries, museums, child-care facilities, all are part of the public's education. Each of
these institutions not only mediates an aspect of culture but relates to all of the others in an educational
ecology mediating the wider culture. Cremin writes,

What is more, these various institutions mediate
the culture in a variety of pedagogical modes and

166

through a range of technologies for the recording, sharing, and distribution of symbols. In effect, they define the terms of effective participation and growth in the society.[28]

The question for Christian religious educators is what role the church plays in this wider ecology and how it relates to the other elements.

For Cremin, education is a primary vehicle by which the public is formed and maintains itself; therefore, discussion about the character of public education is essential for the creation of a public. Too often, he feels, the concentration on the school has ignored the wider ecology and thus has let the education of the public occur uncritically. The result tends to be un-critical socialization and the deterioration of the public. Educators need to ask "What knowledge should 'we the people' hold in common? What values? What skills? What sensibilities?"[29] Without attention to these questions, educators have forgotten their funda-mental purpose of providing the conditions for the transmission and transformation of the culture across the generations.

To counter the narrowness and naivete of the focus on school as education, Cremin suggests that educators think comprehensively about the institutions which carry education, relationally about how they interact, and publically about what they should transmit and in what ways.[30]

To return to the notion of the public church in light of this educational analysis suggests that Chris-tian educators need to be fundamentally concerned with the relation of the church and its education to the culture in which the church finds itself. Christian people are not only educated within the church, for they participate in the broader educational ecology. Unless the church seeks to be a tribe insulated from the world, the church must engage the educational context which is forming persons, and, in turn, those persons need to be given help in negotiating the terrains of their lives in ways that allow Christian faith to be a vital part of their values, skills, and sensibilities.

As this study has demonstrated, Christian educators have often been guilty of a narrowness and naivete simi-lar to their public school counterparts. While many

167

educators have sought to extend the scope of the
church's education, they have in practice more often focused exclusively on the school of the church or elements within the church. The notion of a comprehensive
scope for Christian religious education is still essentially undeveloped. More is needed than an excellent
church school and the coordination of educational elements within the church. Cremin's thinking publicly,
comprehensively, and relationally may be helpful to
Christian educators. Publicly attention must be given
to what of the faith (values, sensibilities, skills,
and symbols) are to be taught and how, and more importantly, how they relate to the faith taught in the
modern world. Fundamentally this is a restatement of
the historic task of Christian apologetics. Moreover,
Christian educators need to think comprehensively about
the institutions which carry religious education, and
relationally about how these institutions interact with
each other and the education of the public. An understanding of the matrix within which Christian education
functions provides an opportunity to engage education
and evangelism in significant ways.

It seems that the world is the context for Christian education, and that the development of the public
church is to be facilitated as a primary task of Christian education. What is crucial here is that neither
the analysis of the church's role in culture, nor a
theological assessment of that situation can be ignored
as has too often been the case in Christian education.
Such a perspective encourages the apologetic and world-
engaging tendencies in Christian education, but it does
so because of theological commitments about the nature
of church. It criticizes a position that allows the
church to ignore the world and accepts that the public
church itself is a community of communities within the
context of still other meaning communities. Simply,
the theological decision here expressed is that the
Christian message is to be in relationship to the world
and responsible for the world, but not to be lost in
the world. To use H. Richard Niebuhr's classical categories: Christ is the transformer of culture.31 The
church in this paradigm must be faithful, but it also
must understand the culture and seek to transform it in
light of the vision of the kingdom of God.

Such an agenda has been "deep in the soul" of
Protestant church education. In the late nineteenth
century, the ecology was so well developed that the

Protestant church was the public church and soul of
American culture. The progressive church educators in
turn recognized the effects of modernity in breaking
up this unitary nineteenth-century ecology. Their
search for the church school was a fundamental search
for a new ecology in the midst of pluralism. Yet, many
of them wrongly thought a coordination of agencies
within the church was sufficient. Coe however sought
to understand the pathways through which an individual
must go to become Christian and the actual role of the
church in relation to culture. Several cultural and
theological shifts ended this search. The future of
Christian education and of the Christian church may rely
on how well the present ecology can be understood and
addressed. Marty has shown that that task will be difficult, but that it is possible within the convictions
and practice, the faith and life, of the emerging public
church.

There has been a consistent thrust in Protestant
education to engage the public and to develop the appropriate ecology for Christian education; yet, factors
have interfered to simplify inappropriately the goal
and to narrow the form to the school and the church.
To recognize these possibilities and tensions, as well as
the inherent inertia is a beginning to setting a viable
Christian education policy for the future.

The perennial tasks of Christian education emerge
in each new social context. Any good form of education
is continually being reformed, and therefore its tasks
must be perennial. In the past there is both direction
for the reformation and evidence of pitfalls to avoid.
In the pluralistic world of today, purpose, form, and
scope draw on the past and are re-made by the present.
The purpose of church education transcends the nursery
of the church to become the education of the public, the
form moves from the school to education, and the scope
embodies a new Christian education ecology.

In accepting this task, the Christian educator, to
borrow a phrase from Cremin and to re-present an important aspect of the tradition, is accepting the task of
prophecy--the calling of the people of God, via criticism and affirmation, to their noblest traditions and
affirmations. It is a calling to struggle to teach in
order that the faith may speak vitally within the
cacophany of pluralism.

Notes

[1]George H. Betts, "Perennial Tasks of Religious Education," *Religious Education* 23 (Special Convention Issue 1928):699-705.

[2]Ibid., pp. 700-704. The continuing importance of these ideas is also reflected in the fiftieth year celebration of the REA at which time William Clayton Bower was asked to assess the state of Protestant religious education. Bower highlighted many of the same concerns as the continuing "inventory of potentials" for Protestant education:
1. professional cooperation in Protestant church education
2. relation of church education theory and practice to modern educational theory
3. integration of religious education into total life of the church
4. relation of religious education to public education.

See Bower, "Protestant Religious Education," *Religious Education* 48 (September-October 1953):307-309.

[3]"Plans for Increasing the Interest and Efficiency," in *Fifth National Sunday-School Convention* (New York: Aug. O Van Lennep, 1872), p. 101.

[4]William Reynolds, "The Whole Field," in *Eighth International Sunday School Convention* (Chicago: Executive Committee, 1896), p. 42. See also William Reynolds, "A Look at the Field," in *Seventh International and World's Second Sunday School Conventions* (Chicago: Executive Committee, 1893), pp. 153-163.

[5]See John Vincent, "A Forward Look for the Sunday School," and A. R. Taylor, "The Relation of the Sunday-School to the Public School," in International Sunday School Association, *The Development of the Sunday School 1780-1905: The Official Report of the Eleventh International Sunday School Convention* (Boston: International Sunday School Association, 1905), pp. 164-173, 185-189.

[6]*A Report of Committee on Education of the International Sunday School Council of Religious Education*, by Walter S. Athearn, Chm. (Kansas City: International Sunday School Council, 1922), pp. 5-12.

[7]Henry C. Trumbull, "Historical Introduction," in *Fifth National Sunday-School Convention*, p. 22.

[8]Henry C. Trumbull, The Sunday School: Its Origin, Mission, Methods, and Auxiliaries (Philadelphia: John D. Wattles, 1888), pp. 171-172.

[9]William Reynolds, "Reports from the Field," in Sixth International Sunday School Convention of the United States and British North American Provinces (Chicago: Executive Committee, 1890), p. 28.

[10]This purpose is stated in many sources. See for example: James A. Worden, "The True Basis of Sunday-School Work," in Second International Sunday School Convention of the United States and British American Provinces (Washington, D.C.: Executive Committee, 1878), pp. 55-61.

[11]Elmer Ellsworth Barnes, "Some Relations of Religious Education and Secular Education," Religious Education 2 (October 1907): 121.

[12]Walter S. Athearn, Religious Education and American Democracy (Boston: Pilgrim Press, 1917), pp. 14-21. See also Walter S. Athearn, A National System of Education (Boston: Pilgrim Press, 1920).

[13]William B. Kennedy, The Shaping of Protestant Education: An Interpretation of the Sunday School and the Development of Protestant Educational Strategy in the United States, 1789-1860 (New York: Association Press, 1966), p. 71.

[14]E. Morris Fergusson, Historic Chapters in Christian Education in America: A Brief History of the American Sunday School Movement, and the Rise of the Modern Church School (New York: Fleming H. Revell Co., 1935), p. 173.

[15]Betts, "Perennial Tasks of Religious Education," p. 700. (The underlining is Betts').

[16]Kennedy, Shaping Protestant Education, p. 75.

[17]Ibid., p. 76.

[18]See Chapter VI.

[19]William Clayton Bower et al., "The Church as Educator: A Body of Source Material Which Reveals the Way in Which the Churches Conceive Their Educational Function," Religious Education 22 (April 1927):370, 376.

[20]For an understanding of competing ecclesiologies, see Avery Dulles, Models of the Church (Garden City: Doubleday & Co., 1974).

[21]Dwayne Huebner, "Education in the Church," Andover Newton Quarterly 12 (January 1972):123.

[22]The same is true for many other church educators. Vincent, Cope, Bower, and Athearn also attempted to bridge these areas of human inquiry. However, the task of integrating theology and the human sciences, the practical theology task, is extremely difficult. Too often the subtleties and contradictions tend to be ignored.

[23]Martin E. Marty, The Public Church: Mainline--Evangelical--Catholic (New York: Crossroad Publishing Co., 1981), p. 3.

[24]Ibid.

[25]Ibid., pp. 87-93.

[26]See Sidney E. Mead, The Old Religion in the Brave New World: Reflections on the Relation between Christendom and the Republic (Berkeley: University of California Press, 1977).

[27]Lawrence A. Cremin, Public Education (New York: Basic Books, 1976), pp. 21-22. See also Idem, Traditions of American Education (New York: Basic Books, 1977), pp. 123-126.

[28]Cremin, Public Education, pp. 22-23. For a description of how these institutions interact to enable public decision making see Peter L. Berger and Richard J. Neuhaus, To Empower People: The Role of Mediating Structures in Public Policy (Washington, D.C.: American Enterprise Institute for Public Policy Research, 1977).

[29]Cremin, Public Education, p. 74.

[30]Ibid., pp. 57-97.

[31]See H. Richard Niebuhr, <u>Christ and Culture</u> (New York: Harper & Row, 1951).